DATE DUE

BRODART, CO.   Cat. No. 23-221

Field Guides to Finding a New Career

Engineering, Mechanics, and Architecture

The Field Guides to Finding a New Career series

Field Guides to Finding a New Career

Engineering, Mechanics, and Architecture

By Kelly Wiles

Ferguson Publishing
An imprint of Infobase Publishing

Field Guides to Finding a New Career: Engineering, Mechanics, and Architecture

Copyright © 2010 by Print Matters, Inc.

Ferguson
An imprint of Infobase Publishing
132 West 31st Street
New York, NY 10001

Library of Congress Cataloging-in-Publication Data

Wiles, Kelly.
    Engineering, mechanics, and architecture / by Kelly Wiles. — 1st ed.
        p. cm. — (Field guides to finding a new career series)
    Includes bibliographical references and index.
    ISBN-13: 978-0-8160-7996-4 (hardcover : alk. paper)
    ISBN-10: 0-8160-7996-X (hardcover : alk. paper)
1. Engineering—Vocational guidance.
2. Architecture—Vocational guidance.
3. Mechanics, Applied—Vocational guidance. I. Title.
    TA157.W495 2009   620.0023—dc22

                                                    2009027910

Ferguson books are available at special discounts when purchased in bulk quantities for businesses, associations, institutions, or sales promotions. Please call our Special Sales Department in New York at (212) 967-8800 or (800) 322-8755.

You can find Ferguson on the World Wide Web at http://www.fergpubco.com

Produced by Print Matters, Inc.
Text design by A Good Thing, Inc.
Illustrations by Molly Crabapple
Cover design by Takeshi Takahashi
Cover printed by Bang Printing, Brainerd, MN
Book printed and bound by Bang Printing, Brainerd, MN
Date printed: April 2010
Printed in the United States of America

10 9 8 7 6 5 4 3 2 1

This book is printed on acid-free paper.

Contents

Introduction: Finding a New Career

Today, changing jobs is an accepted and normal part of life. In fact, according to the Bureau of Labor Statistics, Americans born between 1957 and 1964 held an average of 9.6 jobs from the ages of 18 to 36. The reasons for this are varied: To begin with, people live longer and healthier lives than they did in the past and accordingly have more years of active work life. However, the economy of the twenty-first century is in a state of constant and rapid change, and the workforce of the past does not always meet the needs of the future. Furthermore, fewer and fewer industries provide bonuses such as pensions and retirement health plans, which provide an incentive for staying with the same firm. Other workers experience epiphanies, spiritual growth, or various sorts of personal challenges that lead them to question the paths they have chosen.

Job instability is another prominent factor in the modern workplace. In the last five years, the United States has lost 2.6 *million jobs*; in 2005 alone, 370,000 workers were affected by mass layoffs. Moreover, because of new technology, changing labor markets, ageism, and a host of other factors, many educated, experienced professionals and skilled blue-collar workers have difficulty finding jobs in their former career tracks. Finally—and not just for women—the realities of juggling work and family life, coupled with economic necessity, often force radical revisions of career plans.

No matter how normal or accepted changing careers might be, however, the time of transition can also be a time of anxiety. Faced with the necessity of changing direction in the middle of their journey through life, many find themselves lost. Many career-changers find themselves asking questions such as: Where do I want to go from here? How do I get there? How do I prepare myself for the journey? Thankfully, the Field Guides to Finding a New Career are here to show the way. Using the language and visual style of a travel guide, we show you that reorienting yourself and reapplying your skills and knowledge to a new career is not an uphill slog, but an exciting journey of exploration. No matter whether you are in your twenties or close to retirement age, you can bravely set out to explore new paths and discover new vistas.

Though this series forms an organic whole, each volume is also designed to be a comprehensive, stand-alone, all-in-one guide to getting motivated, getting back on your feet, and getting back to work. We thoroughly discuss common issues such as going back to school, managing your household finances, putting your old skills to work in new situations, and selling yourself to potential employers. Each volume focuses on a broad career field, roughly grouped by Bureau of Labor Statistics' career clusters. Each chapter will focus on a particular career, suggesting new career paths suitable for an individual with that experience and training as well as practical issues involved in seeking and applying for a position.

Many times, the first question career-changers ask is, "Is this new path right for me?" Our self-assessment quiz, coupled with the career compasses at the beginning of each chapter, will help you to match your personal attributes to set you on the right track. Do you possess a storehouse of skilled knowledge? Are you the sort of person who puts others before yourself? Are you methodical and organized? Do you communicate effectively and clearly? Are you good at math? And how do you react to stress? All of these qualities contribute to career success—but they are not equally important in all jobs.

Many career-changers find working for themselves to be more hassle-free and rewarding than working for someone else. However, going at it alone, whether as a self-employed individual or a small-business owner, provides its own special set of challenges. Appendix A, "Going Solo: Starting Your Own Business," is designed to provide answers to many common questions and solutions to everyday problems, from income taxes to accounting to providing health insurance for yourself and your family.

For those who choose to work for someone else, how do you find a job, particularly when you have been out of the labor market for a while? Appendix B, "Outfitting Yourself for Career Success," is designed to answer these questions. It provides not only advice on résumé and self-presentation, but also the latest developments in looking for jobs, such as online resources, headhunters, and placement agencies. Additionally, it recommends how to explain an absence from the workforce to a potential employer.

Changing careers can be stressful, but it can also be a time of exciting personal growth and discovery. We hope that the Field Guides to Finding a New Career not only help you get your bearings in today's employment jungle, but set you on the path to personal fulfillment, happiness, and prosperity.

How to Use This Book

Career Compasses

Each chapter begins with a series of "career compasses" to help you get your bearings and determine if this job is right for you, based on your answers to the self-assessment quiz at the beginning of the book. Does it require a mathematical mindset? Communication skills? Organizational skills? If you're not a "people person," a job requiring you to interact with the public might not be right for you. On the other hand, your organizational skills might be just what are needed in the back office.

Destination

A brief overview, giving you an introduction to the career, briefly explaining what it is, its advantages, why it is so satisfying, its growth potential, and its income potential.

You Are Here

A self-assessment asking you to locate yourself on your journey. Are you working in a related field? Are you working in a field where some skills will transfer? Or are you doing something completely different? In each case, we suggest ways to reapply your skills, gain new ones, and launch yourself on your new career path.

Navigating the Terrain

To help you on your way, we have provided a handy map showing the stages in your journey to a new career. "Navigating the Terrain" will show you the road you need to follow to get where you are going. Since the answers are not the same for everyone and every career, we are sure to show how there are multiple ways to get to the same destination.

Organizing Your Expedition

Fleshing out "Navigating the Terrain," we give explicit directions on how to enter this new career: Decide on a destination, scout the terrain, and decide on a path that is right for you. Of course, the answers are not the same for everyone.

Landmarks

People have different needs at different ages. "Landmarks" presents advice specific to the concerns of each age demographic: early career (twenties), mid-career (thirties to forties), senior employees (fifties) and second-career starters (sixties). We address not only issues such as overcoming age discrimination, but also possible concerns of spouses and families (for instance, paying college tuition with reduced income) and keeping up with new technologies.

Essential Gear

Indispensable tips for career-changers on things such as gearing your résumé to a job in a new field, finding contacts and networking, obtaining further education and training, and how to gain experience in the new field.

Notes from the Field

Sometimes it is useful to consult with those who have gone before for insights and advice. "Notes from the Field" presents interviews with career-changers, presenting motivations and methods that you can identify with.

Further Resources

Finally, we give a list of "expedition outfitters" to provide you with further resources and trade resources.

Make the Most of Your Journey

Winston Churchill once said, "We shape our buildings, thereafter they shape us." Since the human race began, this has been true; as time passes, we make our systems, structures, and products more advanced, thus advancing ourselves as a civilization. Those who work in engineering, mechanics, or architecture have some of the most important and exciting jobs because their work is at the forefront of this advancement. These forward-thinking professions are concerned with creating ways for our rapidly growing population to progress while continuing to live and thrive on our planet.

While attention to detail is important in these careers, attention to the big picture is also important. To find success, you must be able to think big—not just about how your work will affect those around you now, but how it will affect the future of the human race as a whole. Employers, clients, and other professionals will be excited to work with you if they can tell that you are genuinely interested in making the world a better place, and that you are able to think on a large enough scale to do so.

If you want to pursue a career in engineering, mechanics, or architecture, you have to love the work, and also be patient on your path to job success. As famed architect Frank Lloyd Wright once said about his chosen field, "I know the price of success: dedication, hard work, and an unremitting devotion to the things you want to see happen." Just because you have a knack for gardening does not mean you will necessarily become a successful landscape architect overnight; if drawing maps is a hobby of yours, it does not mean you possess all the necessary skills to work as a professional cartographer just yet. In order to work in many of these job fields, you must be licensed, and you must sometimes obtain educational degrees before even applying to take the licensure exams. Just think about it the next time you are driving over the Golden Gate Bridge: aren't you glad the structural engineers involved in its design were required by law to know exactly what they were doing? Dedication and extreme enjoyment of the work at hand will help see you through these at-times tedious requirements. If you are incredibly passionate about design, then taking some design classes to become legitimately qualified will be enjoyable learning experiences as opposed to mundane stepping-stones to be fulfilled in your career pursuit.

If you love what you do, you will also be able to find enjoyment even in the most stressful parts of your job. Financial motivation alone will not sustain you through long hours and difficult projects. Your paycheck will be steady for the most part, and you may even advance to a high-paying salary, but you should not pursue a career in engineering, mechanics, or architecture only because you are aiming to get rich. As the surveyor profiled in Chapter 5 of this book explains, "If you want a guaranteed million bucks, this profession is probably not yours. Not that it is impossible to get there from here, it is just less likely than, say, owning a casino." Professionals who find success in engineering, mechanics, or architecture are people whose priorities lie more in environmental issues and human interests than in financial gain and material wealth.

The chance to employ creativity is another part of what can make working in engineering, mechanics, or architecture so satisfying. Though practical knowledge is necessary in these career fields, so is imagination. The various professionals who are profiled in these book chapters were asked why they were drawn to their field. Here are some of their answers:

☞ "It allowed me to get creative and let my artistic side come out," says Misti, the drafter profiled in Chapter 6.
☞ "I saw it as a way to experience the results of my design efforts," says Tim, the broadcast and sound engineering technician profiled in Chapter 8.
☞ "I loved art and design," says Kim, the landscape architect profiled in Chapter 4.

While Misti, Tim, and Kim may not be considered professional artists, they may definitely be considered artistic professionals in what they do. Artistic and visual abilities are valued as much as the knowledge of scientific and mathematic principles. Although computer design software programs have become vital tools in the design process nowadays, the ability to put a pencil to paper and create an accurate sketch of something is at the root of the visualization skills necessary for any career in engineering, mechanics, or architecture.

Most of these professions have been around since the dawn of our civilization. In 3000 B.C.E., the Egyptian Land Register orchestrated the construction of the pyramids. Studies have proven that Stonehenge was mapped out by prehistoric surveyors who used pegs and ropes as measurement tools. Although the tools may have changed over the years, the objective in these careers has remained the same: progress. Coming up with a new design concept or a breakthrough idea has always been an exhilarating reward for the hours of calculations, measurements, and research involved in any project, from cartographer Amerigo Vespucci's early sketches of America to the Apple design team's invention of the first iPod.

With the possibility for large-scale success, however, comes the possibility for large-scale failure. Take for example Boston's "Big Dig" project, the single most expensive highway project in the history of the United States. What began as a thrilling revelation in a city's transportation layout turned into a financial and constructional disaster. Poor planning, research, communication, and instruction among those involved resulted in the Dig going way over budget and schedule, and inconveniencing an entire city for over a decade. When the project was supposedly finished, one of the tunnels collapsed. Though there were many professionals working on the Big Dig, it was the engineers who got the most public portion of the blame for the project's failure. Even if the job is on a smaller scale, the field of engineering demands you be aware of the amount of responsibility you will be taking on and the people that you will be affecting with your designs. For instance, creating a faulty footpath layout on a college campus will not inconvenience an entire city, but it will still inconvenience an entire school, and it will not do much for your reputation as a landscape architect. No matter what scale you are working on, your end product will be a success only if you have been meticulous and thorough in all aspects of the planning phase, and aware of the human element of the design.

Another part of engineering, mechanics, and architecture that can be both rewarding and challenging is the teamwork aspect of the work you do. Scientists, government officials, urban planners, city councils, construction workers, and environmental organizations are just a few examples of the various people that may be involved in a project you are hired to work on. An industrial production manager must be able to speak the language of the company executives *and* the assembly line workers in order to make sure that production requirements are effectively met by both sides. As a drafter, you must be able to compromise with an architect when your design model does not accurately represent the original drawing. Although there may be personality clashes or differences of opinion to contend with from time to time, it can be extremely satisfying when you and those you are working with are able to successfully come up with a solution for a difficult project. "There is nothing better," says Art, the industrial designer profiled in Chapter 7, "than being part of a passionate team trying to make a groundbreaking product."

The key to breaking into your chosen career in engineering, mechanics, or architecture is to prove to your potential employers that you are just what Art the industrial designer says: passionate. If you have always drawn maps in your spare time and been fascinated by geography, then you are already a passionate cartographer-in-the-making; if you work at an auto body shop but have always been obsessed with airplanes, then your passion for aircraft mechanics is waiting to emerge. Right now you are already passionate about your future career—more passionate than a lot of younger people who jump into jobs in the field right out of college without considering that it might not be what they want to do. This can work to your advantage. When you enroll in degree programs, attend informational seminars, or apply for jobs, your potential employers and mentors will take you more seriously. They will know that you have had experience in the working world and have not chosen your new career field on an undergraduate whim.

Once you have decided to pursue a career in engineering, mechanics, or architecture, the first thing you need to do is to find out exactly what the requirements are for working in your profession in your state. The national organizations or unions that represent your career field can provide you with this information; most of it is readily available on their Web sites. Links to these sites are provided in each of the chapters in this book, but do not depend completely on the Internet to map out the steps in your career path. Call one of the contact numbers provided on the site and consult with someone about which educational or certification programs they would recommend for someone with your particular career experience. Ask around and find someone you can talk to who works in your career field. Most people are flattered to be asked for advice by someone just starting out, and having a mentor on your side is always an extra confidence-booster.

You will bolster your résumé and better your chances of employment after completing an educational program if you try and find some work in your field while you are still learning about it. You may have a hard time getting paid to work if you are not qualified yet, so seek out unpaid internships or volunteer opportunities in your field. If you prove that you are ready to learn and enthusiastic about the work even without a paycheck attached, then potential employers will be more likely to hire you into a substantial position once you have obtained the appropriate credentials because they know you are driven and committed. The payoff on your end will be future employment contacts, valuable on-the-job-training, and some work experience to put on your résumé. Be friendly. Be humble. And speak up if you have an idea! Employers in these fields value ingenuity and are always looking for new solutions to old problems.

If you are a few decades past college age, then the idea of starting a new career can be especially intimidating. However, you should think of it this way: you have a head start on the freshman just beginning at square one. You have probably already acquired some of the knowledge you need to work in your new career field. You probably do not need to take Mathematics 101 all over again; you just need to dust off your calculator and brush up on your skills with a refresher course. The important thing in changing careers a little later in life is to keep an open mind and be able to keep re-educating yourself, especially where technology is concerned. You will be more attractive to potential employers if you demonstrate that you are eager to become knowledgeable about the latest digital programs or computer software, that you read the latest news in the field, and that you are not stuck in the technological dark ages. Be willing to listen to new ideas and take instruction from people who might not have had as much working-world experience as you have.

The road to a career in engineering, mechanics, or architecture may be long and strenuous. Once you have gotten there, the work can be extremely challenging. But if you are passionate about helping to turn the wheel of human progress, the satisfaction you will get out of your career will be immeasurable. Think big, look forward, and prepare to embark on a thrilling and rewarding career journey.

Self-Assessment Quiz

I: Relevant Knowledge

1. How many years of specialized training have you had?
   - (a) None, it is not required
   - (b) Several weeks to several months of training
   - (c) A year-long course or other preparation
   - (d) Years of preparation in graduate or professional school, or equivalent job experience

2. Would you consider training to obtain certification or other required credentials?
   - (a) No
   - (b) Yes, but only if it is legally mandated
   - (c) Yes, but only if it is the industry standard
   - (d) Yes, if it is helpful (even if not mandatory)

3. In terms of achieving success, how would you rate the following qualities in order from least to most important?
   - (a) ability, effort, preparation
   - (b) ability, preparation, effort
   - (c) preparation, ability, effort
   - (d) preparation, effort, ability

4. How would you feel about keeping track of current developments in your field?
   - (a) I prefer a field where very little changes
   - (b) If there were a trade publication, I would like to keep current with that
   - (c) I would be willing to regularly recertify my credentials or learn new systems
   - (d) I would be willing to aggressively keep myself up-to-date in a field that changes constantly

5. For whatever reason, you have to train a bright young successor to do your job. How quickly will he or she pick it up?
    (a) Very quickly
    (b) He or she can pick up the necessary skills on the job
    (c) With the necessary training he or she should succeed with hard work and concentration
    (d) There is going to be a long breaking-in period—there is no substitute for experience

II: Caring

1. How would you react to the following statement: "Other people are the most important thing in the world?"
    (a) No! Me first!
    (b) I do not really like other people, but I do make time for them
    (c) Yes, but you have to look out for yourself first
    (d) Yes, to such a degree that I often neglect my own well-being

2. Who of the following is the best role model?
    (a) Ayn Rand
    (b) Napoléon Bonaparte
    (c) Bill Gates
    (d) Florence Nightingale

3. How do you feel about pets?
    (a) I do not like animals at all
    (b) Dogs and cats and such are OK, but not for me
    (c) I have a pet, or I wish I did
    (d) I have several pets, and caring for them occupies significant amounts of my time

4. Which of the following sets of professions seems most appealing to you?
    (a) business leader, lawyer, entrepreneur
    (b) politician, police officer, athletic coach
    (c) teacher, religious leader, counselor
    (d) nurse, firefighter, paramedic

5. How well would you have to know someone to give them $100 in a harsh but not life-threatening circumstance? It would have to be...
    (a) ...a close family member or friend (brother or sister, best friend)
    (b) ...a more distant friend or relation (second cousin, coworkers)
    (c) ...an acquaintance (a coworker, someone from a community organization or church)
    (d) ...a complete stranger

III: Organizational Skills

1. Do you create sub-folders to further categorize the items in your "Pictures" and "Documents" folders on your computer?
    (a) No
    (b) Yes, but I do not use them consistently
    (c) Yes, and I use them consistently
    (d) Yes, and I also do so with my e-mail and music library

2. How do you keep track of your personal finances?
    (a) I do not, and I am never quite sure how much money is in my checking account
    (b) I do not really, but I always check my online banking to make sure I have money
    (c) I am generally very good about budgeting and keeping track of my expenses, but sometimes I make mistakes
    (d) I do things such as meticulously balance my checkbook, fill out Excel spreadsheets of my monthly expenses, and file my receipts

3. Do you systematically order commonly used items in your kitchen?
    (a) My kitchen is a mess
    (b) I can generally find things when I need them
    (c) A place for everything, and everything in its place
    (d) Yes, I rigorously order my kitchen and do things like alphabetize spices and herbal teas

4. How do you do your laundry?
    (a) I cram it in any old way
    (b) I separate whites and colors

(c) I separate whites and colors, plus whether it gets dried

(d) Not only do I separate whites and colors and drying or non-drying, I organize things by type of clothes or some other system

5. Can you work in clutter?

(a) Yes, in fact I feel energized by the mess

(b) A little clutter never hurt anyone

(c) No, it drives me insane

(d) Not only does my workspace need to be neat, so does that of everyone around me

IV: Communication Skills

1. Do people ask you to speak up, not mumble, or repeat yourself?

(a) All the time

(b) Often

(c) Sometimes

(d) Never

2. How do you feel about speaking in public?

(a) It terrifies me

(b) I can give a speech or presentation if I have to, but it is awkward

(c) No problem!

(d) I frequently give lectures and addresses, and I am very good at it

3. What's the difference between *their, they're,* and *there*?

(a) I do not know

(b) I know there is a difference, but I make mistakes in usage

(c) I know the difference, but I cannot articulate it

(d) *Their* is the third-person possessive, *they're* is a contraction for *they are*, and *there* is a deictic adverb meaning "in that place"

4. Do you avoid writing long letters or e-mails because you are ashamed of your spelling, punctuation, and grammatical mistakes?

(a) Yes

(b) Yes, but I am either trying to improve or just do not care what people think

    (c)   The few mistakes I make are easily overlooked

    (d)   Save for the occasional typo, I do not ever make mistakes in usage

5.   Which choice best characterizes the most challenging book you are willing to read in your spare time?

    (a)   I do not read

    (b)   Light fiction reading such as the Harry Potter series, *The Da Vinci Code*, or mass-market paperbacks

    (c)   Literary fiction or mass-market nonfiction such as history or biography

    (d)   Long treatises on technical, academic, or scientific subjects

V: Mathematical Skills

1.   Do spreadsheets make you nervous?

    (a)   Yes, and I do not use them at all

    (b)   I can perform some simple tasks, but I feel that I should leave them to people who are better-qualified than myself

    (c)   I feel that I am a better-than-average spreadsheet user

    (d)   My job requires that I be very proficient with them

2.   What is the highest level math class you have ever taken?

    (a)   I flunked high-school algebra

    (b)   Trigonometry or pre-calculus

    (c)   College calculus or statistics

    (d)   Advanced college mathematics

3.   Would you rather make a presentation in words or using numbers and figures?

    (a)   Definitely in words

    (b)   In words, but I could throw in some simple figures and statistics if I had to

    (c)   I could strike a balance between the two

    (d)   Using numbers as much as possible; they are much more precise

4.   Cover the answers below with a sheet of paper, and then solve the following word problem: Mary has been legally able to vote for exactly half her life. Her husband John is three years older than she. Next year,

their son Harvey will be exactly one-quarter of John's age. How old was Mary when Harvey was born?
(a) I couldn't work out the answer
(b) 25
(c) 26
(d) 27

5. Cover the answers below with a sheet of paper, and then solve the following word problem: There are seven children on a school bus. Each child has seven book bags. Each bag has seven big cats in it. Each cat has seven kittens. How many legs are there on the bus?
(a) I couldn't work out the answer
(b) 2,415
(c) 16,821
(d) 10,990

VI: Ability to Manage Stress

1. It is the end of the working day, you have 20 minutes to finish an hour-long job, and you are scheduled to pick up your children. Your supervisor asks you why you are not finished. You:
(a) Have a panic attack
(b) Frantically redouble your efforts
(c) Calmly tell her you need more time, make arrangements to have someone else pick up the kids, and work on the project past closing time
(d) Calmly tell her that you need more time to do it right and that you have to leave, or ask if you can release this flawed version tonight

2. When you are stressed, do you tend to:
(a) Feel helpless, develop tightness in your chest, break out in cold sweats, or have other extreme, debilitating physiological symptoms?
(b) Get irritable and develop a hair-trigger temper, drink too much, obsess over the problem, or exhibit other "normal" signs of stress?
(c) Try to relax, keep your cool, and act as if there is no problem
(d) Take deep, cleansing breaths and actively try to overcome the feelings of stress

3. The last time I was so angry or frazzled that I lost my composure was:
    (a) Last week or more recently
    (b) Last month
    (c) Over a year ago
    (d) So long ago I cannot remember

4. Which of the following describes you?
    (a) Stress is a major disruption in my life, people have spoken to me about my anger management issues, or I am on medication for my anxiety and stress
    (b) I get anxious and stressed out easily
    (c) Sometimes life can be a challenge, but you have to climb that mountain!
    (d) I am generally easygoing

5. What is your ideal vacation?
    (a) I do not take vacations; I feel my work life is too demanding
    (b) I would just like to be alone, with no one bothering me
    (c) I would like to do something not too demanding, like a cruise, with friends and family
    (d) I am an adventurer; I want to do exciting (or even dangerous) things and visit foreign lands

Scoring:

For each category...

For every answer of *a*, add zero points to your score.
For every answer of *b*, add ten points to your score.
For every answer of *c*, add fifteen points to your score.
For every answer of *d*, add twenty points to your score.

The result is your percentage in that category.

Civil Engineer

Civil Engineer

Career Compasses

Get your bearings on what it takes to become a successful civil engineer.

Mathematical Skills in order to make the technical calculations necessary to a project's design (30%)

Relevant Knowledge of the different factors involved in the construction of a project, and how each one affects the others (25%)

Communication Skills to be able to clearly convey ideas and design concepts to the various people involved in a project (25%)

Ability to Manage Stress in a job field that demands strict adherence to deadlines, the ability to problem solve under pressure, and constant multitasking (20%)

Destination: Civil Engineer

We have come to expect a lot from our modern lives. We expect subway cars to transport us to our destination. We expect our roads not to flood when it rains. We expect bridges not to collapse when we drive over them. We are able to take these expectations for granted thanks to the careful planning of a civil engineer.

In short, civil engineers make things work. They figure out how the infrastructures we use, and the structures we build, can be designed to function effectively. Civil engineers use their knowledge of scientific and mathematic principles, and their understanding of economic and environmental factors, to plan and oversee a project's design and construction. Usually, civil engineers are hired to work on large-scale projects that will affect many people.

In addition to designing new projects, civil engineers are also hired to help upgrade existing ones. As the world's population increases, the systems we depend on—such as water supply, waste management, and transportation networks—must be adjusted. More people in the world means increased pollution and fewer natural resources to go around. It is a civil engineer's job to figure out how we can function and progress as a civilization without depleting our planet's resources, which is why job opportunities in this field are plentiful even during times of economic crisis. In fact, employment in civil engineering is predicted to grow by 18 percent over the course of the next decade.

Essential Gear

Contact information for your state's licensing board. The requirements to apply for an engineering license vary according to state. You can find out the specific components and requirements for your state's licensing exam by contacting the licensing board in your state. The contact information can be found here: http://www.ncees.org/licensure/licensing_boards.

Although certain civil engineers (usually referred to as "site" engineers) oversee all aspects of a project, most civil engineers work in one specialized discipline. There are six major civil engineering disciplines: Structural engineering focuses on how structures such as buildings, tunnels, and bridges can be designed to support themselves, and to withstand wear and tear. Construction engineering deals with overseeing all aspects of a project's construction; duties range from developing project sites to evaluating supplies to drafting employment contracts. Water resources engineering focuses on the methods of managing and collecting water as a natural resource. Environmental engineering (formerly known as sanitary engineering) focuses on pollution control, waste management, recycling systems, and the public health issues that may potentially arise from flaws in these facilities. Transportation engineering focuses on planning, constructing, and maintaining the infrastructures that get people from here to there, such (as roadways, trains systems, airports, water ports, and subway systems. Geotechnical engineering focuses on how rocks, soil, terrain, and other geological components of the planet influence our infrastructures.

A civil engineer's duties on a project vary depending on the particular discipline. If you are a geotechnical or environmental engineer, a lot of your work may be done outside, researching a project site's landscape or soil alongside a surveyor. If you are a construction engineer you might work both outside troubleshooting construction problems and inside writing plan specifications and contracts. For urban projects, part of your duties might include meeting with city administrators to discuss certain factors such as drainage codes, zoning regulations, pollution control laws, and community consensus results.

Essential Gear

Fundamentals of Engineering Supplied-Reference Handbook. Once you are ready to begin preparing, the study materials for the first of the two licensing exams (the Fundamentals exam) can be found in this standard handbook. You can buy it in a bookstore or order it online at http://www.ncees.org/exams/study_materials.

As a civil engineer in any discipline, you must be both practical and creative. You must possess practical knowledge about scientific and mathematic principles, but be imaginative enough to apply these existing principles toward new design solutions. You must also have good communication skills, as the construction of large-scale projects depends upon the collaboration of many different people. You must also be good with details, deadlines, and multitasking in order to make sure that the different facets of a design plan will work together.

Unlike an architect, who usually designs a single building that will affect a limited number of people, a civil engineer designs infrastructures that can affect entire cities. Overseeing projects on such a large scale puts an immense amount of pressure on the engineer to succeed. If a project fails, you can be held at fault, and in the worst cases, you could be charged with criminal negligence. If a project runs over budget or schedule, or a design needs re-thinking, you must be willing to put in extra hours to find solutions for these problems. It is up to you as a civil engineer to make sure that everyone else involved in a project's completion is not wasting his or her efforts on a faulty design. Civil engineering is a lot of responsibility, and you must be very confident in your abilities and tirelessly dedicated to your work. On average, civil engineers work a standard 40-hour week; however, their schedule is subject to change depending on certain phases of construction. A civil engineer's salary ranges from $40,000 to $60,000 a year.

Obtaining your civil engineering license is almost as difficult as being a civil engineer, at least in some states. Becoming licensed means passing the Fundamentals of Engineering exam and the Principles and Practice in Engineering exam. Some states have very strict application requirements for these exams, and will not allow you to take the exams unless you have a bachelor's degree in engineering and four years of interning experience. However, application requirements are not always that strict. Some state exam applications accept bachelor's degrees in any field; in other states, as long as you have a few years of engineering experience, you do not need a degree to apply for the exams. Also, some exams are state specific. For example, in order to become a licensed engineer in California, you must take an additional exam about earthquake engineering, no matter what engineering discipline you will be working in. Before you do anything else, find out what the exam requirements are for your state. Find out how much more academic credit or work experience (if any) you need in order to apply to take your state's licensure exams. Knowing exactly how many steps stand between you and your engineering license is the first step towards becoming a professional civil engineer.

You Are Here

Civil engineers must strike a balance between the practical and the creative.

Do you have a strong background in science? Remember those science projects you used to do in grade school? Civil engineering is like that, only on a much bigger scale. Even the most creative ideas and the most interesting design concepts rely on basic scientific and mathematic principles in order to work. If a career in civil engineering interests you, it is probably because science and math are strengths of yours, and you probably already employ them a fair amount in your current job field. Even if an engineering degree is not required to obtain an engineering license in your state, it would be a good idea to take a few courses to brush up on your science skills before you take the licensure exams.

Do you enjoy discovering new solutions to old problems? A civil engineer is someone who is devoted to progress. The most successful civil engineers are the ones who are not afraid to keep learning. As civilization evolves, its systems must evolve, which means that a civil engineer's education is never really complete. The best civil engineers are continually re-educating themselves on new technologies and discoveries. When a problem arises during a project, the best civil engineers do not get frustrated—they thrill to the challenge of finding a solution to the problem.

Are you personable and do you work well as part of a team? Cooperation is imperative to the construction of large-scale projects. Many different people in many different fields are involved, and civil engineers must feel comfortable talking to all of them. If you are an intern or a student trying to gain experience in the field, be friendly and respectful to make sure that the supervisors on that project will remember you as someone they want for their next project. Though civil engineering is about using scientific principles and coming up with creative solutions, another part of the job is making a good impression on the people you are working with.

Navigating the Terrain

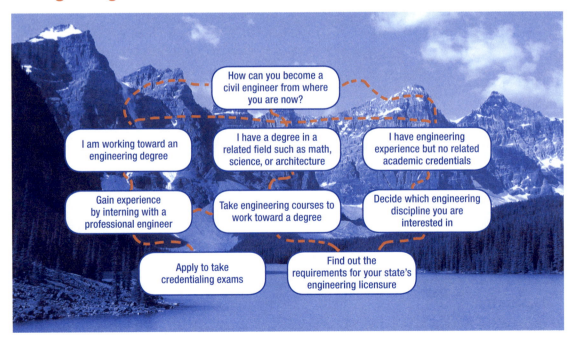

How can you become a civil engineer from where you are now?

I am working toward an engineering degree

I have a degree in a related field such as math, science, or architecture

I have engineering experience but no related academic credentials

Gain experience by interning with a professional engineer

Take engineering courses to work toward a degree

Decide which engineering discipline you are interested in

Apply to take credentialing exams

Find out the requirements for your state's engineering licensure

Organizing Your Expedition

Before you set out, know where you are going.

Decide on a destination. Consider your own particular strengths and decide which type of civil engineering you are interested in (structural, construction, water resources, environmental, transportation, or geotechnical). Though it is possible to obtain a degree in general engineering, your career path will be easier to follow if you know the discipline in which you will specialize. Check out the latest civil engineering magazines and Web sites to get informed on the various branches of civil engineering, and figure out which one suits you the best.

Scout the terrain. Once you have decided which civil engineering discipline is right for you, it is time to figure out how to get licensed. The best place to start is the American Society of Civil Engineering. There are ASCE branches all over the country that hold informational seminars open to members and non-members alike. Attending ASCE seminars will put you in touch with civil engineers who can give you advice on which engineering programs and internships would help you on your way to licensure in your particular state. Check out the ASCE Web site (http://www.asce.org) to find out about seminars in your region. As long as you register (which usually requires a small fee), you are welcome to attend.

Find the path that's right for you. Obtaining your civil engineering license may seem like a long, intimidating process, especially if you are lacking in education or experience in the field. It is important to create a realistic plan for yourself, taking into account certain factors in your life such as finances, children, or time availability. Are you able to commit to a four-year fulltime engineering program at an accredited university? If the answer is no, there are still ways to complete the necessary requirements for the licensing exams. Online courses can get you an engineering degree. Weekend volunteering on public projects can count as experience. Ask an ASCE member to put you in touch with a working civil engineer whose lifestyle is similar to yours, and ask them for tips on how they were able to manage their schedule before they got licensed.

Notes from the Field

Colin Harris, PE, LEED AP
Civil engineer, self-employed under the name "Iowa Center"
Minneapolis, Minnesota

How did you get started in civil engineering?

I entered college unsure about which major seemed most appealing to me. My interests included art and music, as well as math and science. Since the engineering curriculum at Brown University required the highest number of mandatory classes of any major I was considering, I decided to start down that route at the beginning of my freshman year. After graduation I immediately pursued full time civil engineering employment because I was eager to enter a less theoretical environment and work on real-world projects.

Why did you want to get into civil engineering?

I have always had a fascination with buildings, trains, cars, and transit networks. I had considered directing my expertise more toward architecture or community planning; however, I believed that having a scientifically based civil engineering background would be the most useful and interesting to me as I began to practice within the professional design arena. I felt that by combining my training in engineering with my natural abilities in the arts, I would be able to create unique

Landmarks

If you are in your twenties . . . If licensure in your state does not require a bachelor's in engineering, you still may want to better your chances of passing the engineering exams by taking a class or getting an internship under a professional engineer. At this age, chances are you are up for change and amenable to relocating for a job, so if your state does require an engineering degree for licensure, you might want to consider relocating to a state that will allow you to take the licensure exam without one. If you cannot relocate, you should enroll in some engineering courses at a local university (or online) to find out whether *projects and be able to effectively collaborate with a diverse range of professional design teams.*

How did you break in?

My first job after college was with a civil engineer with whom I had worked as an intern after my freshman year. He was just getting started with his own engineering business by the time I was graduating and invited me to work with him during the beginning phases of the new business. Having developed a professional relationship early on in my college career made it easier to break into the work environment upon graduation, and from that point, I was able to jump off and be able to choose my next phases.

What are the keys to success in your career?

Anyone can learn engineering methods, but having sensitivity, patience, and respect are critical for developing long-lasting relationships with both clientele and coworkers. These qualities are proving to be very important to me and allow me to build new bridges (figuratively) and keep them intact throughout my career, wherever I may be and whatever I may be doing. Also it is important to know the value of deadlines, because this is a universal concept and no matter how big or small they may be, meeting them consistently is one of the best opportunities to show your dedication to your clients and your design team.

or not you want to take the plunge and devote the next four years to getting your bachelor's in engineering.

If you are in your thirties or forties . . . A lot of people with degrees in math or science end up working in civil engineering. If your experience lies in these fields, you should look into getting a master's degree in engineering. If you do not have time to commit to enrolling at a university, there are some great online programs, such as Penn Foster College and Norwich University, that offer accredited engineering degrees of both the two- and four-year variety. You can find information about these programs at the Guide To Online Schools Web site: http://www.

guidetoonlineschools.com. If you have a solid background in skills that are relevant to the field of civil engineering (anything math or science related, or experience in construction, land maintenance, or road work), sometimes a year or two of engineering experience will qualify you to take the state exams. Volunteering is a good way to start getting this experience. The American Society of Civil Engineers holds many conferences and community service meetings all over the country, and they are always in need of volunteers (both paid and unpaid) to help with project planning and construction. Go to their Web site to find out about volunteer opportunities in your area and get involved.

If you are in your fifties . . . If you are interested in civil engineering but do not have the time to go back to school full time to obtain the credentials necessary to take the licensure exams, that is okay. Licensure allows you to work on your own, under the job title of professional engineer, but you can still find fulfilling work in the field even if you are not licensed. Your years of job experience and previous education may qualify you to offer your services to a professional engineer. Look into engineering firms in your area, talk to someone who works in the field, or contact someone at the American Society of Civil Engineers to find out what work or volunteering you might be qualified for.

If you are over sixty . . . Public projects that affect a community are large endeavors, and no matter what age you are, or what kind of experience you have, there are always volunteer opportunities on these kinds of projects. Contact the American Society of Civil Engineers, or talk to someone you know in the engineering field, to find out who you should contact to volunteer in your area.

Further Resources:

The Web site **iCivil Engineer** is the go-to Internet source for all things civil engineering. It is a great place to learn about the past, present, and future of the field, with historical facts, current headline news, and image galleries. http://www.icivilengineer.com

The **National Council of Examiners for Engineering and Surveying** is the best place to find information on how to obtain your engineering license. The site gives you the particulars on state licensure requirements, exam study materials, and helpful links to check the status of your exam application.   http://www.ncees.org

Civil Engineering magazine, available both in print and online, is the first and foremost civil engineering publication. It reports on new projects and advancements in the field, and covers all different civil engineering disciplines.   http://www.pubs.asce.org/magazines/CEMag

Aircraft Mechanic

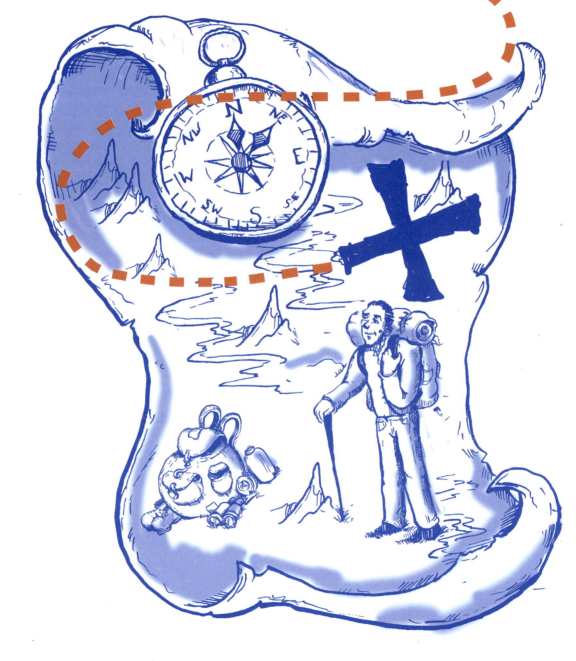

Aircraft Mechanic

Career Compasses

Get your bearings on what it takes to be a successful aircraft mechanic.

Relevant Knowledge of the various technological, mechanical, and electrical aspects of aircraft function (30%)

Ability to Manage Stress in a pressurized job that can be both physically uncomfortable and mentally demanding (30%)

Organizational Skills in order to keep track of maintenance records and inspection schedules (20%)

Caring about details and being meticulous enough to work overtime to solve especially complicated issues (20%)

Destination: Aircraft Mechanic

Airplanes have come a long way since they were invented in the early 1900s. The idea of flying high above the earth in a winged metal box is no longer a strange and dangerous concept, but simply a routine part of modern travel. However, though some people are more comfortable on airplanes than others, you would be hard-pressed to find a person who has not felt at least a little bit nervous during a bumpy flight. Everyone has heard the airplanes-are-safer-than-cars statistic. Another helpful reminder for fearful flyers may be that in order to fly, every single plane must be rigorously inspected by someone who knows planes inside and out. This person is called an aircraft mechanic. An aircraft mechanic is responsible for making sure that an airplane is in safe working condition. Aircraft mechanics use mechanical expertise, technical knowledge and physical skill to examine, test, and, if necessary, repair the various functions of an aircraft. Everything from the landing gear to the air conditioning inside the cabin must meet the safety standards of the Federal Aviation Administration for a plane to be allowed to fly.

Essential Gear

The Aviation Mechanic Handbook. The best, most popular reference guide for anyone in the field of aircraft mechanics. It features formulas, diagrams, charts, lingo and more, and fits inside a toolbox. It is available on Amazon.com.

Those interested in becoming aircraft mechanics should keep abreast of the latest developments in avionics systems, as these systems increasingly improve upon an aircraft's function. However, although technology has had an effect on an aircraft's capabilities, most of an aircraft mechanic's job duties cannot be done by a computer. For this reason, employment rates in the field are expected to remain steady. There is even a slight employment increase predicted over the course of the next decade, as more people with capabilities in the job field are choosing college over technical school, leaving mechanical positions open. Another tip on bettering your job options is to seek initial employment at smaller, more regional airlines, where employment opportunities are always greater.

As an aircraft mechanic, your job duties include inspection of different equipment inside the airplane such as the engine or brakes, or different parts of the actual airplane body such as the tail or the wings. To perform an inspection, an aircraft mechanic uses tools that can range from a simple wrench to tighten a bolt, to a complicated magnetic x-ray system to scan a plane's fuselage for cracks. Part of the job involves maintaining written records of a plane's repair history and maintenance schedules. Aircraft mechanics must routinely meet with pilots and troubleshoot additional problems based on a pilot's descriptions of possible aircraft issues. Aircraft mechanics sometimes work indoors, in a hangar or in a repair facility, but can often be called to do last-minute repairs outside on the runway. Like most professions in the field of aviation, aircraft mechanics work in shifts, usually eight hours at a time, 40 hours a week. Weekend hours are common.

Most aircraft mechanics specialize in a certain type of aircraft, such as helicopters or jets, or specialize in a certain part of an aircraft, such as the body or the electrical system. The field can be further broken down into a few other categories. Power plant mechanics do mainly engine and propeller work. Airframe mechanics work on everything but the engine and propeller. As the job title suggests, combination airframe-and-power plant mechanics (A&P mechanics) work on both. Avionics technicians work mostly with an aircraft's electronic systems.

In order to become a successful aircraft mechanic, you must be able to perform well under stress. Unexpected mechanical issues or technical malfunctions may arise at the last minute and you must be able to remain calm and focused while working against the clock to solve the problem. Like any other type of mechanic dealing with the various parts of a complex operating system, you must be detail-oriented and thorough in your inspection. You must be adaptable, be willing to maintain a flexible schedule, and capable of taking instruction from different kinds of people.

Essential Gear

Contact information for the union in your area. There are a few different unions that defend the job rights of aircraft mechanics. Protect yourself and your career by having their number(s) in your phonebook. The Aircraft Mechanics Fraternal Association is also a resource for career support and advice. Their contact information is available at: http://amfanational.org.

Being called out to the runway to examine a technical malfunction on a plane full of waiting passengers is not what you would call a stress-free job. The restlessness of those aboard the aircraft and the impatience of the workers on the ground can be incredibly stressful factors in an aircraft mechanic's work. Aside from the pressure of keeping a timely flight schedule, the pressure of making sure that an entire aircraft is set to fly safely puts a tremendous burden of responsibility on the aircraft mechanic. In addition to the mental stress of the job, the physical stresses can also be trying. While troubleshooting a problem, aircraft mechanics must often twist their bodies into awkward, uncomfortable positions, stand on ladders, or remain outside for long periods of time in freezing temperatures.

Though aircraft mechanics occasionally begin working without completing an educational program, most attend a specialized school in order to learn the skills necessary to the job field. The Federal Aviation Administration requires approximately 18 to 24 months of school, which is not that long when you consider the educational requirements for some professions. Educated or not, once you do begin working as an uncertified mechanic, you are only allowed work under the supervision of someone who is certified. This is a good way to enter the profession, and will provide you with valuable on-the-job-training. Eventually you will most likely want to become certified in order to better your job prospects and increase your salary. Getting certified means passing written, oral, and on-site tests. There are also work experience and training requirements that vary depending on what type of certification you are aiming for. To obtain a power plant or airframe certificate, you need to have had either had 18 months of work experience or have completed an educational program at a certified school. To obtain a combined power plant and airframe certificate, you must have had 30 months of work experience. The Federal Aviation Administration also has strict policies in order to make sure that aircraft mechanics keep their skills current. Certifications must be renewed, and some mechanics are required to undergo 16 hours of training every 24 months.

You Are Here

Gauge your skills for a career as an aircraft mechanic.

Do you have a strong background in mechanics or carpentry? Are you the type of person who enjoys fixing your own car or bike? Do you have experience as a plumber or carpenter? If you are handy with tools, then you have already picked up some basic skills that will prove valuable in the field of aircraft mechanics. Though you will have to educate yourself on the technologies specific to aviation, if you are already adept at other kinds of mechanical endeavors, you have a head start in your pursuit of a career as an aircraft mechanic.

Do you enjoy physical activity and being outdoors? As an aircraft mechanic, you work out on the runway or in airplane hangars or repair shops. You employ bodily strength and flexibility to perform your job duties. In other words, it is not a typical office job, which is why some are drawn to the field. While the job can be tiring, you will find your work as an aircraft mechanic rewarding if you enjoy physical activity.

Do you work well under pressure? Do you perform better when you are under a deadline than you do when left to your own devices? The ability to buckle down and focus when the clock is ticking is an important characteristic for an aircraft mechanic to possess. Having a lot of people depending on you to fix an equipment malfunction can be stressful, but if you are a successful mechanic, this pressure can actually give you added motivation to complete the task efficiently.

Organizing Your Expedition

Before you set out, know where you are going.

Decide on a destination. In order to know where you are going, you have to decide where you want to end up. As previously discussed, the field of aircraft mechanics can be broken down into a few different specializations. Consider your particular strengths, experience, and interests. Are you more interested in working on an airplane's frame and exterior, its engine, or its electronic instruments? As you gain experience

Navigating the Terrain

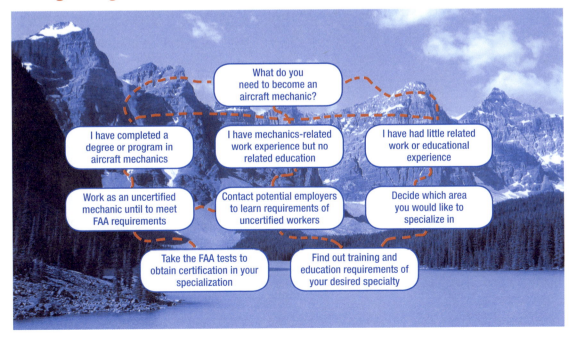

What do you need to become an aircraft mechanic?

I have completed a degree or program in aircraft mechanics

I have mechanics-related work experience but no related education

I have had little related work or educational experience

Work as an uncertified mechanic until to meet FAA requirements

Contact potential employers to learn requirements of uncertified workers

Decide which area you would like to specialize in

Take the FAA tests to obtain certification in your specialization

Find out training and education requirements of your desired specialty

Notes from the Field

Carl Violette
Director of corporate aircraft maintenance
MassMutual Financial Group
Springfield, Massachusetts

How did you get started as an aircraft mechanic?

I enlisted in the army thinking helicopters were going to be the "buses" of the future. Little did I know how much they cost to operate. While in the service one of the individuals in my platoon introduced me to the FAA requirements for being a mechanic as a civilian. I purchased many of the books and started preparing while still in the army. Once out, I enrolled at the mechanics school in Bedford, Massachusetts.

Why did you want to get into aircraft mechanics?

I actually enjoy very much the puzzle-solving aspect of aircraft maintenance. I have found that many of the best troubleshooters also enjoy either crossword or Sudoku puzzles. It gives me great satisfaction to have returned an aircraft to service and see it leaving on its next trip.

How did you break in?

I actually was offered an airline job right out of school, but when told I would have to relocate and work third shift, I decided to pass. I

or education in the field, you may change your mind, but it is a good idea to at least begin thinking about what kind of mechanics you may be good at.

Scout the terrain. While doing your own research is important, the best way to figure out the first step on your career path is to talk to someone who has been working in the career field for a while. Contact someone at the Aircraft Mechanics Fraternal Organization and ask to be put in touch with a working mechanic in your area, or better yet, go to an airport near you and in person and ask to talk to someone who can answer your career questions. Talking to an actual professional in the field is a good way to get advice on how to go about fulfilling the started at a small aircraft operation that was trying to start up an airline with small piston-powered aircraft. The pay was very low, but I was given some good experience. Then I got a job on the second shift at the largest airport in the area. We worked on everything from small piston aircraft to the airliners. This was great experience and was where I met my next employer. This was a Fortune 100 corporation that had both helicopters and jets and I ended up working for them for 20 years.

What are the keys to success in your career?

Early in my career I had the wrong model. It was not until I learned the hard way that results are what people are looking for. Effort will only take you so far. Effort without results will get you fired. Once I started focusing on results, my career took off. Aviation, unlike many fields, has no tolerance for mistakes. Set high goals for quality and safety, then figure out how to keep the aircraft flying. Putting in some overtime just comes with the territory. Lastly, document when you are saving the company money. With the amount of money required to keep aircraft flying, your employer will appreciate you more when you can show the amount you save them.

educational and work experience necessary for certification. If you are qualified to begin doing uncertified mechanic work, talk to a few potential employers to find out what kind of job opportunities are out there.

Find the path that's right for you. There are various paths that lead to a career as an aircraft mechanic. Maybe you have been working in a mechanics-related field and are qualified to obtain certification right away. Or maybe you are not ready for certification just yet and need to get a year of entry-level work experience to figure out what specialization you are interested in. Be realistic in planning your career, and also your career environment. If you are not interested in living in a large city, then set your sights on a smaller, more local airport.

Landmarks

If you are in your twenties . . . Check out Collegebound.net to find out what FAA-certified programs are available in your area. It might be a good idea to take an online math course or two to brush up on your mathematics skills before applying. If you are planning on searching for jobs right away, consider relocating. At this point in your life, you probably have not fully settled down yet and are willing to move, which is an advantage. There are always more jobs at smaller airports in more rural areas. Even if you eventually want to live in a large urban area, you can hone your skills and build your résumé by working as an uncertified mechanic at a local airport for a year or two.

If you are in your thirties or forties . . . Though you will still need to gain aircraft-specific work experience under a certified mechanic in order to become certified yourself, any previous experience you have had in a mechanics-related field will be useful in finding employment. One way to get a feel for the field is to visit the Aircraft Mechanics Forum online. There are many professionals who post regularly on the forum and would be willing to offer advice on transitioning from your current career into the field of aircraft mechanics.

If you are in your fifties . . . Check out the Industry Events page on the Aircraft Maintenance Technology Society Web site. Attend a conference in your area to meet professionals in the aviation industry. Even if you are not certified, if you have the appropriate skills and a fair amount of work experience, and you show an enthusiasm for the field of aviation, you will be able to find a mentor who can help point you in the direction of odd jobs or volunteer opportunities.

If you are over sixty . . . Even if you are not in a condition to perform physical tasks like you used to, your knowledge and experience with mechanics or airplanes may qualify you for less physically strenuous work in the field of aircraft mechanics. Contact someone at the Aircraft Maintenance Technology Web site to find out what kind of work you are qualified to do. Another place that may be able to put you in touch with potential employment contacts is the American Society of Aviation Artists (http://www.asaa-avart.org).

Further Resources

The **Aircraft Mechanics Forum** is a place to post questions about anything at all related to the field of aircraft mechanics. This is a great way to connect to people of all levels and qualifications who are working in the field.   http://www.aircraftmechanic.org

Aircraft Maintenance Technology magazine is a publication of the society of Aviation Maintenance Professionals. The online magazine has all the latest news and technological developments in the field of aircraft mechanics.   http://www.amtonline.com

The Federal Aviation Administration (FAA) is responsible for requirements and professional certification. Their extensive Web site provides up-to-date information on developments not only in mechanics but in every other aviation-related field as well.   http://www.faa.gov

Cartographer

Cartographer

Career Compasses

Get your bearings on what it takes to become a successful cartographer.

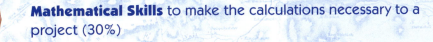

Mathematical Skills to make the calculations necessary to a project (30%)

Relevant Knowledge about computer systems and the most recent technological developments (30%)

Caring about aesthetics and the artistry involved in mapping (20%)

Organizational Skills in order to compile and fact-check a variety of measurements and data (20%)

Destination: Cartographer

Close your eyes and picture America. What do you see? Most likely you are imagining the 48 contiguous states, their various shapes fitting together like puzzle pieces. In actual fact, the states are one giant landmass, but most of us imagine them as separate sections with outlined borders. In other words, we imagine our country the way a cartographer has drawn it. This process involves more than just putting a pencil to paper and sketching an area of land. Before creating a map, cartographers must gather a wide variety of information, both spatial data (such as latitude or longitude) and nonspatial data (such as rainfall). The cartographer uses scientific knowledge, mathematic principles, and visualization techniques to figure out how the information he or she has collected can be accurately represented in a drawing. Like many professions, the field of cartography is changing as technology advances. Sophisticated tools such as Light Imaging Detection and Ranging (LIDAR) and Geographic Information Systems (GIS) have become an integral part of the mapping process. The growing popularity of the Internet has increased the need for technologically savvy cartographers. Keeping oneself (and one's computer) updated on the latest developments in cartographic technology has become a necessary element to career success.

There are two main categories of cartography. General cartography involves basic maps such as road maps or atlases. Thematic cartography involves maps that are drawn to illustrate specific pieces of information, such as population density or trends in crop formations. Some cartographers specialize in one category and others do both. There are also people working in the field whose jobs qualify them as something slightly different than just a cartographer. A map editor fact-checks to make sure that the scale, measurements, and other information on the finished map are completely accurate. Photogrammetrists assess distances and measurements in photographs of various areas. Mapping technicians work under a cartographer or photogrammetrist, compiling data and calculations. Work environments are

Essential Gear

Geographic information system software.
This software collects, stores, analyzes, and displays geographic data. It is a must-have for any cartographer. An excellent resource for those learning how to use the software is the book *Mapping Hacks: Tips and Tools for Electronic Cartography.* This go-to guide to GIS technology provides 100 easy techniques for using GIS software to draw maps.

equally as varied. Some cartographers work for firms, and some are self-employed. In addition to map companies, your client list may include oil and gas companies, construction firms, and branches of government such as the Federal Emergency Management Agency, the U.S. Forest Service, or the Bureau of Land Management.

A bachelor's degree in cartography is the standard qualification to enter the field, but a bachelor's degree in a related discipline such as engineering, geography, or computer science is also acceptable. If you have a degree in an unrelated field, gaining experience via interning or volunteering is a good way to better your job prospects. Some people start out as mapping technicians before becoming professional cartographers. If you do not have a bachelor's degree, it would be a good idea to look into two-year programs related to cartography, either at an accredited university or online. A few states have begun requiring that cartographers possess a surveying license; however, most do not. If you are interested in becoming a photogrammetrist, check out the voluntary certification program on the Web site for The American Society for Photogrammetry and Remote Sensing.

Essential Gear

A dependable compass. Even though computer software has replaced the old-fashioned compass, no self-respecting cartographer would be without one of these. It will be useful in any on-site mapping research you may need to do. Find the compass that suits you at The Compass Store at http://www.thecompassstore.com.

Becoming a certified photogrammetrist involves fulfilling work experience requirements and passing an exam.

In order to become a successful cartographer, you must not only possess knowledge in mathematics, science, and geography, but also be skilled at visualization in order to apply that knowledge to design concepts. You must be patient and detail-oriented, willing to go back and check your work until you are sure it is completely accurate, as people rely on maps to be precise. Organization is a key component to cartography, as the job involves funneling many different pieces of information into one succinct whole. Unlike a surveyor, whose spends a lot of time collecting data on site, a cartographer is able to access the information he or she needs from a desk indoors. Modern day cartographers rarely leave the office, and sometimes do not even visit the areas they are mapping. You may devote some time to phone conversations or fax exchanges with surveyors and other professionals involved in the project, and you might occasionally employ a drawing board, but most of your time is spent in front of a computer. There you receive measurement data via e-mail, conduct Internet research, and use tools such as a geographic information system (GIS) to transform your research information into a map design.

The physical demands of cartography are therefore the same as any desk job. The only hazards lie in eye or wrist strain from looking at a computer screen, or back problems from sitting at a desk chair for long periods of time. Mentally, the job is more overtly stressful. The consequences of making even the tiniest of mistakes on a map can cost you your job, or, in the worst cases, result in a lawsuit. A cartographer must be extremely focused and mentally alert at all times, willing to put in the effort it takes to find the most precise measurements. The work can be laborious, which is why you must be dedicated to it. The current salary for cartographers ranges from approximately $23,500 to $65,000. Though this is not as much as someone who works in a field such as finance or law, for those who enjoy the challenges of charting terrain the benefits of the profession go far beyond the pay.

You Are Here

To begin mapping out your career as a cartographer, start here.

Do you have a background in mathematics? One of the misconceptions about cartography is that it is all about drawing. If you have done some research on the field of cartography, and have decided that you are interested in it as a serious profession, chances are you have above average math skills. You may already employ some kind of mathematics in your current job, and possess knowledge that you will be able to use for the calculations and measurements involved in cartography. If you are capable at math but unsure of whether or not you want to embark on a career that requires a lot of it, it might be a good idea to talk to a professional cartographer to find out just how math figures into the job.

Are you a visual person? Cartography is not a traditional art form, such as sculpture or painting, but there is a definite artistry to it. Though cartographers possess strengths in math, the real reason they get into the field is because they are good at—and passionate about—spatial visualization. If you are thinking of going into the field, it probably goes without saying that you have always been fascinated by maps. Do not worry if you have not studied cartography specifically yet; if you have taken any courses in geography, design, or any sort of art, you have a head start.

Are you organized and meticulous with details? As a cartographer, you are dealing with a lot of different information, which means a lot of

Navigating the Terrain

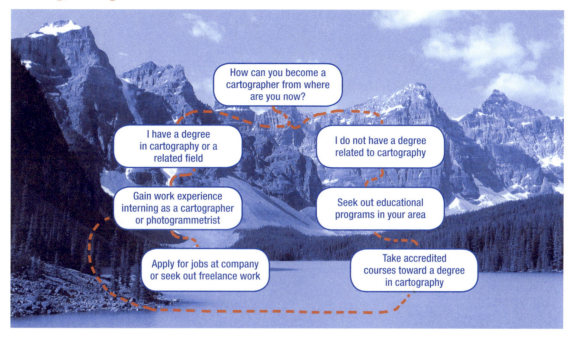

How can you become a cartographer from where are you now?

I have a degree in cartography or a related field

I do not have a degree related to cartography

Gain work experience interning as a cartographer or photogrammetrist

Seek out educational programs in your area

Apply for jobs at company or seek out freelance work

Take accredited courses toward a degree in cartography

room for error. The work can be painstaking at times. However, if you are an organized person by nature you will have a much easier time fulfilling your job duties. This is especially true if you are called upon to prepare several projects at once, which is standard for most firms.

Organizing Your Expedition

Before you set out, know where you are going.

Decide on a destination. Figure out what kind of work you would like to do in the field of cartography. Consider your strengths and interests and decide whether you would rather work in photogrammetry, map editing, or standard cartography. Look into the job details of each career and perhaps talk to someone working in the field to figure out which one suits you best. Think also about the option of working on a freelance basis, or whether you have the marketing savvy—and desire—to start your own business.

Notes from the Field

Kevin W. McCann
Cartographer, Cartographics, LLC
Missoula, Montana

How did you get started as a cartographer/mapping technician?

In the early 1980s, my wife was a degreed cartographer working for the U.S. Forest Service while I was attending vocational school for Computers and Electro-Mechanical systems under the GI bill. After I graduated, we ended up moving to a rural area to live and raise our two young sons. My wife quit her job with the Forest Service and started a cartographic services contracting firm that allowed her to work from home. As my employment opportunities were fairly sporadic at the time, I often helped my wife with the contract map work that continued to come in from the Forest Service. This was still the day of "manual" cartography where one created and edited maps using full-size sheets of specialized materials (mylar, scribecoat, stick-up) to create the plates from which the map layer's negatives would be made and printed maps produced.

Why did you want to get into cartography?

Although the majority of production cartography was still being done "by hand" at this time, computers were beginning to change how maps would be produced in the very near future, and anybody who intended to stay in the business of making maps for long needed to learn and invest in the new digital cartographic processes that were being developed and implemented. With my background in computer technology I was confident that I could transition our present cartographic services contracting business from manual to digital. What I really needed was a better foundation in geography in general and cartography in particular.

Scout the terrain. Find out whether or not your state requires a surveying license for practicing cartographers. If they do not, then you should talk to a cartographer in your area to find out how they got started in the field and what kind of qualifications helped them get jobs. There are also many online cartography forums, such as CartoTalk, that host discussion threads on topics such as how to start as a freelance cartographer, how to work with various design software programs, and recommenda-

How did you break in?

Prior to enrolling in the university to undertake required classes in geography and cartography, I would assist my wife with many of the manual cartography contracts that she had been awarded. This limited involvement with manual map production gave me a basic understanding of map layers, styles, and the processes involved in producing printed maps. While I was still in school, we invested in some basic computer hardware and graphics software and began to pick up small digital mapping projects. A few years later we landed our first completely digital map production contract with the Forest Service.

What are the keys to success in your career?

In addition to having a keen interest in all things having to do with maps, today's successful cartographer will possess a solid understanding of physical geography, digital cartographic techniques, and geographic information systems (GIS), usually as the result of a four-year geography program with a cartography emphasis. It should be noted here that with the advent of geographic information systems, where lines and symbols on a map are no longer simply graphic elements but computerized links to additional feature attributes contained in large geographic databases, there are many GIS professionals who now work almost entirely with geographic databases to perform geographic analysis that may or may not result in the production of an actual map. As a typical map project might include anywhere from 50 to over 100 data layers, more than a dozen font types and symbols with map data being compiled from many different sources and formats in varying coordinate systems and projections, most successful cartographers are fairly well organized in their workflow routines and notes.

tions for online programs. The North American Cartographic Information Society is also a good resource for advice. Visit their Web site at http://dev.nacis.org/?x=16 for contact information.

Find the path that's right for you. In plotting your pursuit of a career in cartography, be realistic about your current schedule and limitations. If you do not have time or income to enroll as a full-time cartography student, there are many other educational options. Also, it is important to be realistic about your reasoning for wanting to enter the field. Some people love drawing maps but do not have the desire or ability to pursue it as a full-time career. There are many organizations and guilds for people who are not professionals and simply enjoy cartography. Even professional cartographic organizations hold seminars that are open to all, professional or not. Consider your goals realistically. If you do not think you are ready to take the plunge to make it your profession yet, you can still edge toward a career by pursuing it first as a hobby.

Landmarks

If you are in your twenties . . . Going back to school is an especially viable option for you at this age. Consider pursuing a four-year degree in cartography or a related field. If your schedule does not permit it, look into online programs. Seek out freelance cartographers in your area and see if you can intern for them. Developing a personal relationship with a mentor can be extremely beneficial to your future career.

If you are in your thirties or forties . . . Many people enter cartography from other job fields. If you have career experience with things such as geography, surveying, design, or computer science, the transition will probably be easier than you think. While you are not required to possess a bachelor's degree in cartography, it is a good idea to take some classes and educate yourself on cartographic technology. Find a cartographer in your area with a similar background to you (kids, finances, education, etc.) and ask them how they went about pursuing their career.

If you are in your fifties . . . You probably have a significant amount of job experience, which is important. You probably also have always been interested in maps. It may be a good idea to enter the field as an avocation first, testing your skills and abilities before plunging headlong into the job market. If you are still committed to making this a fulltime profession, some more intensive computer training will most likely be necessary. Emphasize any past computer experience on your résumé.

If you are over sixty . . . Similar advice for those in their fifties applies to you. Explore the field on a voluntary basis to hone your existing skills. You may try contacting someone at The North American Cartographic Information Society to find out when the next cartography seminar is, and if there are any volunteering opportunities in your area.

Further Resources

CartoTalk is the most extensive cartography forum on the Internet. Questions about any and all aspects of cartography can be answered here by working cartographers from around the globe.   http://www.cartotalk.com
Cartographic Perspectives is the official publication of the North American Cartographic Information Society, and is available online and in print. It is peer-reviewed and accepts map submissions for possible publication.   http://www.cartographicperspectives.wordpress.com
The **North American Cartographic Information Society** maintains a Web site with information such as updates, links, and seminar announcements concerning the world of cartography.   http://www.nacis.org

Landscape Architect

Landscape Architect

Career Compasses

Get your bearings on what it takes to be a successful landscape architect.

Relevant Knowledge of the natural sciences, and the environmental factors they present that will affect the design process (30%)

Caring about environmental issues, and being passionate about finding ways to create eco-friendly designs (25%)

Communication Skills to be able to clearly convey ideas and design concepts to the various professionals and clients involved in a project (25%)

Mathematical Skills in order to make the technical calculations and estimations necessary in the design process (20%)

Destination: Landscape Architect

If you ever had a favorite playground as a kid, or if you have ever taken a jog around the park in your community or stopped to admire the trees on your neighborhood block, then you have paid a compliment to a landscape architect. Regular architects design the buildings we live in, and landscape architects design the world outside of them. As the job title suggests, landscape architects are hired to work on project designs that involve the landscape. Projects range from the small and ornamental, such as designing a footpath around a city reservoir, to the large and functional, such as planning improvements on the layout of a national park. Landscape architects employ creative vision and scientific knowledge to create designs that are not only attractive and practical, but that respect the natural environment.

Essential Gear

Location and address of your local American Society of Landscape Architects (ASLA) branch. Even if you are not yet licensed, you should become familiar with the way the ASLA operates, and attend any seminars you can at your local branch. This will keep you informed on the latest developments in landscape architecture, and also put you in touch with possible mentors and future contacts.

In recent decades, environmental awareness has moved to the forefront of international concern, and landscape architecture has become less about beautifying the landscape and more about preserving it. As the population grows, so does the need for landscape architects who can create design solutions that will allow us to expand as a civilization without depleting our natural resources. The field is becoming increasingly important, and employment rates are predicted to increase by 16 percent in the next decade, faster than most other occupations. A passion for the landscape, both aesthetically and environmentally, is what inspires someone to pursue a career in the field of landscape architecture. Successful landscape architects possess a wide range of scientific knowledge about natural landscape, as well as a creative vision as to how it can be improved upon. Communication skills are extremely valuable for a landscape architect to have, as a large part of the design process is conferring with the different people involved in the project.

As a landscape architect, your job skills lend themselves to many different kinds of projects. You might be hired to work on environmental remediation issues such as the restoration of damaged wetlands or the reclamation of toxic areas (referred to as "brown fields"). If your skills lie more on the decorative side, you may work on projects such as highway beautification, or the layout of trees on a college campus. Landscape architects design various projects for a wide variety of people. Landscape architects can be hired to work on private projects for individual clients, but they can also be hired by clients in the public domain such as historical societies, environmental organizations, real estate developers, town planning boards, or branches of government.

During the early stages of a project, landscape architects spend a lot of their time on site. There they draw sketches, take photographs, and make notes on the existing landscape. If the project deals with environmental preservation, preliminary research may include observing sunlight patterns, conducting studies on climate change, or consulting with geologists and soil engineers. On more urban projects, research may include assessment of existing structural designs, observation of traffic flow, or meeting with city officials or building project architects. After gathering the preliminary onsite research, most of your work as a landscape architect is done in an office. There, site reports, cost estimates, and a project proposal are written. At first, design ideas are usually conveyed by freehand drawings, and once those have been approved by the client (and in certain cases the public officials overseeing the project), more detailed design documents and construction specifications are created using computer-aided design (CAD). CAD has come to play an instrumental role in the work of a landscape architect.

Most landscape architects' salaries fall between $35,000 and $95,000 a year. The majority work for large firms, which means a steady paycheck, fairly regular hours, and health benefits. However, a significant amount (nearly 20 percent) of landscape architects are self-employed. Self-employed landscape architects have the freedom to make their own schedule, but in order to find work, they must be very good at marketing themselves. Landscape architects who work for firms do not have to market themselves as much, but working for firm-assigned clients presents its own challenges. A difficult client who makes unreasonable demands can make the workday twice as long. Landscape architecture requires a good deal of patience, as you may have to put in overtime to please finicky clients, or start a design over again if construction plans are not working. Sometimes clients can be reluctant to reimburse a firm for redesigning, especially if their contract with the firm is for a set fee.

Essential Gear

Landscape Architect Registration Exam (LARE) study materials. There are many different Web sites and manuals that can help you prepare for your licensure exam, which consists of five different sections and involves both multiple choice questions and a graphic component. The LARE breakdown is explained in full here: http://www.testprepreview.com/lare.htm. One of the most popular LARE study guides is a book that can be ordered from this Web site: http://www.mo-media.com/lare.

In order to enter the field of landscape architecture, you must first obtain your landscape architect's license. This means registering for and passing the Landscape Architect Registration Exam. The standard registration requirement is a bachelor's degree in landscape architecture, plus one or two years of work experience, but most states are not quite so cut and dry with their academic requirements. Exam boards will also consider you for exam registration if you have a significant amount of work experience, taken architecture-related undergraduate courses, or completed a technical program in an architectural field. In some states, a personal interview with the landscape architecture board is also a required part of the registration process. Your first step is to find out exactly what your state's requirements are for licensure exam registration. Once you know that, you will know exactly how many more steps lie in between you and a career in landscape architecture.

You Are Here

Landscape architects must be practical, artistic, and environmentally aware.

Do you have a background in design? In the old days, landscape architects used the ancient pencil, paper, and calculator method in their work, painstakingly transcribing each part of their idea into a hand-drawn sketch. Even though computer-aided design has made the process faster, understanding design on a basic level is vital to becoming a successful landscape architect. If you are interested in landscape architecture, you are probably visual person, and you might have a few courses (or a degree) in art under your belt, which is a good start. Even if you have some work experience, and your state does not require a full bachelor's degree in landscape architecture to register for the licensure exams, it is a good idea to take a few architectural design courses to brush up on your design skills before applying.

Do you feel passionately about environmental issues? Scientific and artistic knowledge are definitely valuable strengths to have, but the major reason that most people become involved in the field of landscape architecture is because they care about the environment. Aesthetics and functionality in a design are important to clients, but the underlying reason that landscape architects are hired is to find eco-friendly design solutions. The most successful landscape architects are driven by their desire to make the world a more sustainable place to live.

Are you personable and do you work well with other people? If you are considering becoming a landscape architect, make sure that you sharpen your people skills, as you will have to deal with a variety of different professionals and clients over the course of your career. Many will have visions for a design project that either do not agree with your vision or are not technically possible. You may need to be able to communicate to demanding company heads that their vision for a walkway does not fit into the budget, or compromise your idea for a tree arrangement to please a finicky private client. Even someone with the most visionary design ideas will not get very far in the field of landscape architecture if they cannot communicate and collaborate well with others.

Navigating the Terrain

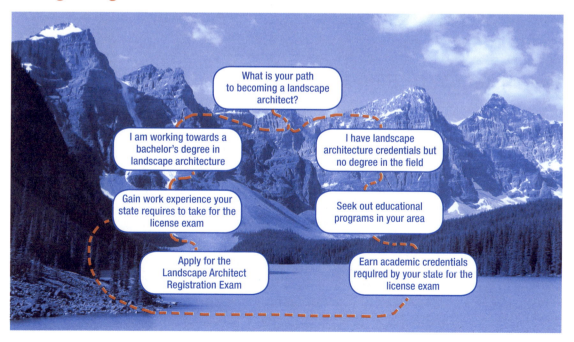

Notes from the Field

Kim Wolf
Vice president for landscape architecture and principal
Rehler Vaughn & Koone, Inc. (RVK Architects)
San Antonio, Texas

How did you get started as a landscape architect?

I majored in landscape architecture at Texas Tech University. My degree in 1980 was "Bachelor of Science in Park Administration with an Emphasis in Landscape Architecture" which is quite a mouthful. The degree at TTU has since become a Bachelor of Landscape Architecture.

Why did you want to get into landscape architecture?

I have always loved being outdoors and recognized early in my college career that I loved art and design but did not want to teach. I took some vocational testing and discovered landscape architecture. I had never heard of the field before, but after the first class I was hooked. I remember feeling like my brain was physically full of new knowledge–it was a great joy to discover a career path that encompassed so much of what I loved (plus a little math).

Organizing Your Expedition

Before you set out, know where you are going.

Decide on a destination. When you visualize your career as a landscape architect, what do you imagine? Do you see yourself working in a firm in the city, or in a home office in a more rural setting? Can you see yourself taking on large-scale environmental remediation projects, or are you more interested in the placement of vegetation in small public parks? Although you should be comfortable working in various settings and on various projects, it is a good idea to know what kind of work environment would fit your lifestyle, and which type of project would be most suited to your strengths. Talk to a few different kinds of landscape architects to get a sense of where you might fit into the field.

How did you break in?

I worked in a different office each summer that I was in college to experience a different aspect of the field. My first job after graduation was with a planning firm in San Antonio. I have been with RVK Architects for 18 years now and it seems like yesterday that I joined the firm. We are a multidisciplinary firm (architects, landscape architects, and interior designers) so we work together as a team to design sustainable projects for our commercial clients.

What are the keys to success in your career?

Communication and adaptation to change. Whether communication is written, spoken, or drawn, you can be the most creative designer in the world, but if you cannot communicate with your clients or your design team, you will be ineffective in your work. And as far as change is concerned, I am the proud owner of a "pass" on the LEED Accredited Professional Exam [a certification of expertise in green building practices]—never stop learning!

Scout the terrain. Once you have thought about what kind of a career you would like to have, it is time to take the first step toward your career goals and figure out how to get licensed. The American Society of Landscape Architects (ASLA) is a good place to start. Their Web site (http://www.asla.org) provides links, addresses, and phone numbers for each state's licensure board. Once you have located your particular state's contact info, visit the Web site of your state's licensure board—or better yet, call the board and ask to speak to someone who can explain to you exactly what steps you need to take in order to apply for your landscape architecture license.

Find the path that's right for you. Obtaining your landscape architecture license may seem like an overwhelming process unless you come up with a realistic plan. If time and money are a concern, then pursuing a four-year bachelor's degree in landscape architecture might be an unrealistic commitment. A better option for fulfilling the academic part of the licensure exam requirement might be a two-year program, either at a technical college, or through online courses. If you need work experience, contact the American Society of Landscape Architects to find out what construction is taking place in your area. Once you have obtained your license, a good resource for job opportunities is the JobLink section on the ASOLA Web site, located here: http://www.asla.org/ISGWeb.aspx?loadURL=joblin

Landmarks

If you are in your twenties . . . At this age, chances are you are not as tied down by familial obligations or time constraint issues, so you may want to consider getting your bachelor's or master's degree in landscape architecture at a university. Take a course or two in landscape architecture to figure out whether or not you want to take the plunge. If you do not have the finances to enroll in a university, there are accredited online courses as well as two-year technical programs that you can take in order to fulfill the academic requirements needed for your licensure exam. It would also be a good idea to acquire some work experience: contact the ASLA to find out what kind of internship positions are available in your area.

Essential Gear

CAD software. If you are going to become a landscape architect, you are going to use computer-aided design software. This Web site offers links to various CAD software programs: http://www.freebyte.com/cad/cad.htm. Ask a mentor in the field which program they recommend for people just starting out.

If you are in your thirties or forties . . . If you work in or have a degree in a field related to landscape architecture (such as art or environmental science), you should look into getting your master's in landscape architecture. If going back to school full time is not a realistic option, look into two-year technical colleges, or consult the directory of online schools (http://www.directoryofonlineschools.com) to find a degree program that will fit into your schedule. If you have had a significant amount of work experience in a related job field, the licensure board may decide that you are qualified enough to take the licensure exam. Talk to someone at your state's licensure board and find out. Even if the board allows you to apply for the exam without the necessary academic requirements, it might be a good idea to take a few design courses anyway to increase your chances of passing the exam.

If you are in your fifties . . . If you have a solid background in a field related to landscape architecture, such as gardening or construction work, you possess skills that are definitely useful in the field of landscape architecture. Public landscaping projects are always in need of volunteers. Contact the American Society of Landscape Architects, or talk to someone you know in the field to find out who you should contact to volunteer in your area.

If you are over sixty . . . If you are a skilled "green thumb" and have maintained gardens on your own property, your skills are easily transferable to the field of landscape architecture. Contact a self-employed landscape architect in your area to find out if you can lend your services to a project they are working on. Also think about reaching out to local community gardens: while not as grandiose as a city or state park, they offer many hands-on opportunities for design.

Further Resources

The **Council of Landscape Architectural Registration Boards** is the best place to find information on how to obtain your architectural license. The site gives you the particulars on state licensure requirements, exam study materials, and helpful contact links. http://www.clarb.org
Landscape Architecture magazine, available both in print and online, is the first and foremost landscape architecture publication. It reports on new projects and advancements in the field, and covers all different facets of landscape architecture. http://archives.asla.org/nonmembers/lam.html
'Pruned' blog is considered one of the best landscape architecture blogs on the Internet. It is a great place to learn about the past, present, and future of the field, with headline news, image galleries, links, and discussion forums. http://pruned.blogspot.com

Surveyor

Surveyor

Career Compasses

Get your bearings on what it takes to become a successful surveyor.

Mathematical Skills in order to make the exact calculations necessary for measurement (30%)

Ability to Manage Stress in a job field that demands mental precision, and also physical labor (25%)

Relevant Knowledge of the technology, scientific principles, and boundary laws used in surveying work (25%)

Communication Skills to be able to clearly convey information to the various people involved in a project (20%)

Destination: Surveyor

Though you consider the earth your home planet, the fact that its surface is 200 million square miles is probably not something that crosses your mind too often. You also probably do not wake up every morning wondering how much dirt there is underneath your house. Most of us do not give much thought to calculations that concern the places we live. The people who do are called surveyors.

A general definition for the verb *survey* is "to examine," and surveyors do just that. Before a structure can be built, a surveyor must examine the proposed project site and produce the measurements and facts necessary for construction. Surveyors are also hired to define boundaries for various areas of land, water, or space. The work of a surveyor involves mathematic abilities, knowledge of property law, and visualization skills. Technology is advancing, and surveying techniques are becoming increasingly sophisticated. Systems such as 3D Laser Scanning, Global Positioning, and Geographic Information are constantly being revamped, allowing for faster, more accurate measurements. There is a growing need for surveyors who can keep informed of the latest technological development. The job field is expected to grow by 21 percent over the course of the next decade, which is much faster than the average of most occupations.

Surveying can be broken down into seven major disciplines. Land surveyors focus on the mapping and measuring of land or proposed project sites, and their work can also include work on bridges or roads. Agricultural surveyors focus on the evaluation and development of rural property, farmland, and wildlife sanctuaries. Quantity surveyors deal chiefly with cost analysis of a building or development project. Construction surveyors are involved with the design assessment, building process, maintenance, and damage repair of construction projects. Geodetic surveyors focus on measuring and mapping the earth's surface and study things such as gravitational pull or tide patterns. Geophysical prospecting surveyors work mostly searching for petroleum deposits under the earth's surface. Hydrographic (or marine) surveyors conduct measurement studies of all things water-related, such as rivers or harbors.

Essential Gear

Surveying flip chart or pocket reference guide. Every surveyor has one of these. It is a quick go-to for information such as mathematical formulas, weather data, and measurement conversion tables you need for surveying calculations on- and offsite. An example of one can be found at http://www.wiley.com.

A surveyor's work environment varies depending on the surveying discipline. As a general rule, surveying is a profession that divides its time equally between onsite and offsite work. Onsite work includes collecting measurements and data using both basic tools, such as surveying rods and measuring tape, or more sophisticated tools, such as Global

Positioning System receivers. It also may include returning to the site to troubleshoot problems once construction is under way. Offsite work may include drawing maps, writing reports and legal documents, and fact-checking research against previous survey results. Surveyors also spend a large portion of time meeting with other professionals working on the project, such as architects or civil engineers, and meeting with the client who has hired them. Government agencies, farmers, and real estate developers are all examples of potential clients.

Essential Gear

The GPS Handbook for Professional GPS users. The Global Positioning System is an important tool in the field of surveying. Even though you are not a professional GPS user yet, it is a good idea to get a head start and familiarize yourself. You can order a copy on the American Congress on Surveying & Mapping Web site here: http://www.acsm.net/newbooks.html.

In order to be successful as a surveyor, you must have strong analytical skills. You need to be able to assess and compare past and present data, and figure out how it will affect the future of a project. You must also be incredibly detail-oriented, and willing to take the time necessary to make sure that your measurements and calculations are precise. The best surveyors have good communication skills: in order to conduct site research alongside other professionals, or to satisfy a client, you must be able to explain your survey findings and how they pertain to the rest of the project in understandable terms.

If you are planning on a career in surveying, you had better be okay with some physical labor. Site research can involve hiking long distances, carrying heavy bags of equipment, or standing for periods of time in extreme heat or cold. You have to be able to perform your job duties under conditions that are sometimes physically uncomfortable. Another challenging part of surveying is the legal aspect of the job. Surveyors can sometimes be called into court to testify in property lawsuits, or, in the worst cases, get sued themselves for faulty calculations. Finally, if you are going to become a professional surveyor you must really love the work: although it offers a steady paycheck and standard hours, surveying does not pay as well as some other professions. The yearly wage of most surveyors falls somewhere between $35,000 and $65,000 a year.

In order to work as a professional surveyor, every state requires that you possess a surveyor's license. Being a licensed surveyor means that you have passed both the Fundamentals of Surveying exam and the Principles and Practice of Surveying exams, with a specified amount of work experience in between. The requirements for applying to these exams vary from state to state. Though a full bachelor's degree in surveying is the fastest way to qualify for the licensure exams, there are alternate ways of fulfilling your educational requirements. Most states will allow you to apply for the exams if you have a bachelor's degree in a field related to surveying, or you have completed a two or three year course of study from an accredited program. In a few states, as long as you have a large amount of work experience, you can apply for the exam with a high school diploma. Find out what the requirements are in your particular state, and use them as a road map to plot your course towards your surveyor's license.

You Are Here

Chart your course to a career as a surveyor.

Do you have a background in mathematics? Measurements and calculations are the name of the game in the surveying field, and if you are interested in becoming a surveyor, chances are you are good at math. You probably already employ some kind of mathematics in your current job field, and possess knowledge that will be useful to you as a surveyor. If you are capable at math but do not use it in your current career, then dust off your calculator and take a refresher course or two before embarking on your surveying degree.

Do you enjoy physical activity? Though surveying does involve some office work, one of the reasons people go into the field is because they do not want a typical "office job," and they like being outside. As a surveyor, you will be getting exercise by simply performing your job duties. If you keep in good shape anyway, then you have a head start. It might be a good idea to volunteer for a surveyor for a day to find out if you are comfortable with the amount of physical labor the job will require.

Are you personable and do you work well with other people? As a surveyor, you need to be able to communicate ideas to and work with all sorts of different people. If you enjoy being part of a team, then you will enjoy the collaborative element that surveying projects require. You will be working with professionals who have different skills than you do, such as architects if you are surveying for a building project or scientists for a land study project. It is important to be able to understand the varying languages and terminology each one uses when discussing the project. If you are just starting out in the field, make sure to be friendly, enthusiastic, and gracious; you never know who will be able to recommend you for future projects.

Organizing Your Expedition

Before you set out, know where you are going.

Decide on a destination. Figure out what type of surveying work you are most interested in. If you live in a rural area with lots of farmland, maybe agricultural surveying would be appropriate. If you are interested in geology, then geodetic surveying would be the field for you. Though all surveyors must pass the same licensure exam, it is important to have

Navigating the T errain

Where would you like to work as a surveyor and how will you get there?

Find out what your state's requirements are for taking the licensure exams

Fulfill educational requirements

Pass the credentialing exam and fulfill work experience requirements

Pass the Principles and Practice of Surveying Exam and apply for jobs

Notes from the Field

Reginald S. Parker
Professional land surveyor, Royal River Survey Company
North Yarmouth, Maine

How did you get started as a surveyor?

I became interested in high school but never worked as a surveyor until I got to college. I was a forestry major at the University of Maine, and took surveying as part of that curriculum. Partially inspired by my survey professor and because I needed a semi-decent income as a young married student, I got a summer job that year in the profession. I continued while in college working part time for a local surveyor and later that year took the LSIT, or "in-training" exam. Upon graduation I went to work full time for a surveying firm in southern Maine as a party chief.

Why did you want to get into surveying?

I was always interested in working outside rather than an "office" job (although the reality is that surveying is about half and half, if you are a small firm like we are). Initially, it was the preference and desire to be involved in a profession where I was not cooped up inside. My interest in history was also fueled by the amount of time spent researching property boundaries, and I found I enjoyed the mystery of solving boundary questions and property rights. And I always enjoyed looking at and studying maps. To me, the work remains fascinating because it involves doing something different almost every day.

How did you break in?

It was not so much breaking into the profession as working within the system. When I was starting in the profession in the early 1970s, in order to eligible to become a licensed professional surveyor one was required to have passed a four-hour state written in-training exam and have served a period of apprenticeship with a licensed practitioner for minimum of three years, performing the various duties involved in dealing with surveying and land transfers. Subsequent to fulfilling those requirements, the taking and passing a second licensing examination was necessary, involving familiarity with the field procedures, mathematics and state boundary law. My survey apprenticeship began in 1971, and I was licensed in 1976. I have been practicing as a professional land surveyor ever since then.

Today the recommended career path includes a degree in surveying or survey/engineering related curriculums through an accredited institution along with a period of apprenticeship, varying in length depending upon specific state requirements for licensure. The University of Maine offers a highly rated curriculum in their Spatial Information Engineering program leading to careers in surveying, GIS, and information technology.

What are the keys to success in your career?

Within the ranks of the profession it is frequently heard that surveyors are a different breed. You have to love the work. Probably because most folks do not like swatting mosquitoes or black flies in places where they grow so thick you literally have to wipe them off the instrumentation before you look through it. Or maybe it is the lack of interest most people have in working outside in zero degree weather. Or soaked to the bone sweating profusely in 110 percent humidity. Boundary survey work involves knowing and understanding how to apply the rules of evidence and boundary law to the evidence one procures through the effort of the fieldwork. Today surveying involves mapping, creating an abstract or symbolic representation of what is found on the face of the earth while using computers, high tech robotics, GPS receivers, scanners, and electronic data collection. It involves the art and science of measurement, of understanding the history of measurement and how the precision of that effort has evolved with time and technology. We tend to be a curious breed, enjoying the challenge of solving the boundary puzzle by applying logic, an understanding of human nature, and rules of law. But the keys to being a successful practitioner within the surveying community, I believe, incorporate the same parallels and common denominators with success in any other profession: understand your client's wishes utilizing good communication skills, keeping your client informed as the project goes forward, staying on top of your business through continuing education, delivering to your client what you agree to deliver when you agree to deliver it. Being honest, forthright, and respectful of those who hire you for your skills along with those whom you hire for their skills. Striving to deliver a product and level of service second to none.

My bottom line is this: Get into surveying, or anything else that you want to pursue, for the love of doing it, for the desire to be the best at what you do. If you want a guaranteed million bucks, this profession is probably not yours. Not that it is impossible to get there from here, its just less likely than, say, owning a casino.

a clear picture of the work you can see yourself doing once you are licensed. Consider your strengths and interests, and do some research to determine what kind of surveyor you would like to be.

Scout the terrain. Once you have given some thought to your surveying goals, it is time to talk to someone from your state's licensing board to find out exactly what you need to do in order to apply for the surveying licensure exams. The Web site for the National Council of Examiners for Engineering and Surveying provides contact and Web site information for the licensing boards in every state. Find it at http://www.ncees.org/licensure/licensing_boards.

Find the path that's right for you. Fulfilling the educational and work experience requirements necessary to take the licensure exams may seem like a long, difficult, and costly process, but it does not have to be if you make a realistic plan for yourself. Talk to a licensed surveyor with a similar background to get tips on how he or she did it. If you have children or financial concerns, then going back to school full time might not be an option. Taking surveying courses from an accredited online program is an affordable option that will allow you to fulfill your educational requirements on your own schedule. Check out the Online Degree Zone Web site (http://www.onlinedegreezone.com) for more information about online courses.

Landmarks

If you are in your twenties . . . Chances are you are amenable to going back to school full time. Even if your state's licensure board does not require a bachelor's degree, you might want to think about obtaining one, as it usually means you will start out in the field with a higher salary. If your schedule will only allow for online courses or a technical program, then get a head start on your work experience requirement. Look into volunteering for a surveying company on the weekends. The fact that you are young and in good shape is a huge plus. It may allow you to take on greater responsibility on a project even though you are not fully educated yet.

If you are in your thirties or forties . . . You are still in good physical condition, and will still be able meet the physical demands of surveying. Look up surveyors in your area and talk to them about possible work opportunities. Getting experience working under a licensed surveyor will allow you to assess whether or not you want to take the plunge into fulfilling the educational requirements necessary to becoming licensed yourself.

If you are in your fifties . . . If becoming a fully licensed surveyor is not a realistic goal for you, look into volunteering opportunities and informational seminars you can attend to learn more about the field of surveying. Check out the Web site for the National Society of Professional Surveyors at http://www.nspsmo.org. There you will find helpful links to surveying projects going on in your area.

If you are over sixty . . . Bear in mind the physical demands of this job before seriously considering a career change. If you are interested in maps and the mapping component of surveying, you may want to look into cartography. While not as physically demanding as surveying, it affords the opportunity to use the mathematical, visual, and geographical skills inherent to the surveyor's trade.

Further Resources

Land Surveyors United maintains a Web site that is chock full of information, links, and advice for all different types of surveying. http://www.landsurveyorsunited.ning.com

American Surveyor magazine is available in print or online. This is the go-to source for keeping up-to-date with all things surveying related. http://www.amerisurv.com

EllenFinkelstein.com is a great resource for help with computer-aided design. Helpful tips, an online store, and links to other CAD-related sites. http://www.ellenfinkelstein.com

Drafter/CADD Operator

Drafter/CADD Operator

Career Compasses

Get your bearings on what it takes to become a successful drafter/CADD operator.

Relevant Knowledge of the CADD system, and other computer programs necessary to creating a design (30%)

Mathematical Skills in order to make the calculations and measurements involved in a design (30%)

Organizational Skills to keep track of the various pieces of information and construction requirements for a particular design (20%)

Ability to Manage Stress in working with others and producing precise measurements and sufficient designs (20%)

Destination: Drafter/CADD Operator

Have you ever played a computer game that allowed you to design and create buildings and towns with the simple click of your computer mouse? If your virtual design was on the road to actual construction, and you were getting paid to create it, then you would be called a drafter. Though an architect is responsible for the initial creation of a project's design, it is the drafter who makes the design visuals come alive. Using computer-aided design and drafting systems, a drafter creates a detailed visualization of the architect's sketch, filling in the blanks so that the design plans are more accessible to clients, construction workers, and others involved in the project. Aside from computer expertise, drafters employ visual abilities, mathematic skills, and knowledge of engineering and construction when they draw up a design.

The computer-aided design and drafting systems are referred to as "CADD," and due to how important these systems have become in the design process, a drafter has also come to be known as a "CADD operator." As technology advances, the CADD systems become more efficient and easy to navigate, which means that there is now less of a need for manual drafting. Those interested in drafting should not only keep up on the latest in CADD technology, but also become knowledgeable in drafting-related fields, such as architecture or engineering. A drafter who can do more than simply operate a CADD system will increase their chances of employment in the job field.

The most common task for drafters involves preparing drawings for buildings or civil works. In the case of buildings, drafters usually work for an architect or a mechanical or electrical engineer. For civil works, drafters work on drawings for civil engineering projects involving infrastructures such as bridges or water systems. Other types of drafters include aeronautical drafters, who work in aircraft-related design, and pipeline drafters, who deal with the layout of places such as oil refineries or chemical plants.

Essential Gear

A solid drafting table. Even with the growing popularity of computer software, and thus the growing usage of regular desks, there are still instances when a drafter must rely on their own drawing abilities, and there is still one of these in every drafting office.

A 40-hour week is standard for most drafters, with some overtime hours when deadlines must be met. Though in some cases a drafter may visit a project site, for the most part drafters work in offices, at desks, in front of computers. Job duties can include drawing up lists of construction specifications, collecting project site data from surveyors or engineers, or calculating cost estimates. However, the primary work a drafter does is with the CADD system, using it to transform the rough sketches of a design into complete construction documents. In order to do this, drafters work continuously with the architect or engineer responsible for the drawing to make sure that the CADD-created design is accurate, as well as to work through changes as the design evolves.

Drafters must be both visually creative and technically informed in order to prepare design drawings that are legible and technically accurate. To become a successful drafter, you must be detail-oriented, as there are many different measurements and data to keep track of. You must also be able to keep abreast of the technological advancements, and willing to continually reeducate yourself on the latest improvements in design software.

The physical challenges of drafting, such as eyestrain, a stiff back, or hand and wrist problems, are the same as most office jobs. The mental challenges are comparable to a lot of office jobs as well, in that you must be able to cooperate with your boss or supervisor. Though being a drafter does involve a certain amount of creative freedom, you are usually working from someone else's idea. If the architect (or engineer) is especially demanding, you may have to put in many extra hours with CADD until you have successfully represented their vision. A drafter can make anywhere from approximately $40,000 to $70,000, but if you advance to senior drafter or start your own drafting company, you can earn more than that. Some drafters eventually become architects themselves, or start their own companies.

Essential Gear

Modern Drafting Practices and Standards Manual. First written in 1901 and updated yearly, this manual is the standard reference guide for drafting lingo, measurements, abbreviations, techniques, and more. Order it here: http://www.draftingzone.com.

Educational requirements are not as black and white in the field of drafting as they are in some other career fields. They depend on what kind of drafting you are doing and what kind of an employer you want to work for. A drafter usually does not have a bachelor's degree in architectural design or engineering. If you have obtained a certificate from a technical institute, taken drafting courses through an online program or a community college, or even received technical training in the Armed Forces, you will be able to find employment opportunities.

Another option is obtaining your drafting certification from the American Design Drafting Association. Though certification is not necessary for employment, passing the Drafter Certification Test is an easy way to prove your qualifications to potential employers. Once you are hired, some employers will help finance continuing education, and you may be able to pursue a higher degree and progress to other positions in the architectural or engineering fields.

You Are Here

Drafters must be visual people and analytical thinkers.

Do you have a background in mathematics? The difference between drawing a virtual structure on a computer game for fun and drawing a virtual structure on CADD for a job is that the latter will actually be built. Actual calculations are needed in order for construction to be successful. This means that if you want to be a drafter, it is not enough to be simply good at visualization and design; you must also be proficient in mathematics. If your skills are rusty, it might be a good idea to take a math course or two to brush up before enrolling in drafting courses.

Do you enjoy working with computers? As a drafter, CADD is your best friend. You spend most of your working hours using its system to create designs and figure out measurements. If you are a drafter who loves your job, then you are a person who loves computers. For successful drafters, figuring out how a new computer program works is exciting rather than annoying. Though a good drafter is definitely skilled in pencil-and-paper sketches, their computer skills are what they employ most on the job.

Are you good at working with others? Drafting involves collaborating with an architect, engineer, and other professionals on a project. While you may give some input of your own, you are mostly working to realize someone else's design idea. Cooperation and listening abilities are important qualities in a drafter. Your work will be much easier if you are able to work well as part of a group.

Navigating the Terrain

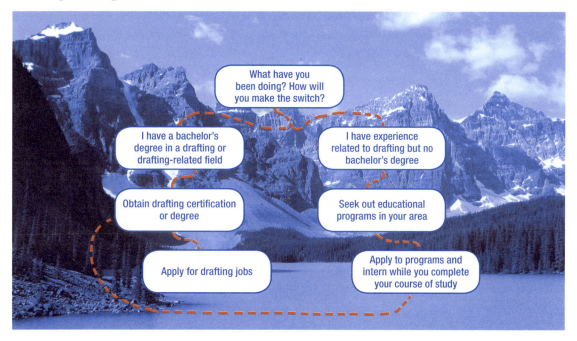

- What have you been doing? How will you make the switch?
- I have a bachelor's degree in a drafting or drafting-related field
- I have experience related to drafting but no bachelor's degree
- Obtain drafting certification or degree
- Seek out educational programs in your area
- Apply for drafting jobs
- Apply to programs and intern while you complete your course of study

Organizing Your Expedition

Before you set out, know where you are going.

Decide on a destination. Consider your end goals in the field of drafting. Are you satisfied to work as a drafter for a larger company? Do you want to start your own company someday? Do you want to eventually become an architect or engineer? Even if you do not yet know for sure, keeping your sights on the future will make your present career path easier to navigate. If you know where you want to go, you will know what steps you need to take in order to get there.

Scout the terrain. Now it is time to do some research. If you have decided that you need a bachelor's degree and want to go back to school full time, look into accredited universities to find out more about how much they cost and what their degree requirements are. If you are inter-

Notes from the Field

Misti Life
Owner and senior drafter, Florida Style Professional Drafting Service
Merritt Island, Florida

How did you get started in drafting?

After high school I was torn between two majors: interior design and graphic design. I went to the local college in Melbourne, Florida, Keiser College (now Keiser University), and I sat down with the career counselor and she and I discussed what vision I had for my future. I told her that I love art and I love to create and design. When I took the enrollment exam she said the exam determined I would have been best suited for the CADD program. I was reluctant at first. But once I started taking the classes and saw the unlimited possibilities CADD offered I was hooked.

Why did you want to get into drafting?

I was drawn to drafting when I was in college I loved that you could create anything with in CADD from a stick figure to a fully engineered high-speed rail system. The college I attended taught us different fields of drafting: mechanical, electrical, civil, and architectural. I found that I enjoyed the civil drafting more than the others because it allowed me to get creative and let my artistic side come out.

How did you break in?

While in college I went to work for a major corporation as a CADD technician. I was there about a year, then I went to work for an en-

ested in two-year technical programs or community college, look into schools or online programs and compare them. Contact the American Design Drafting Association to get information on the Drafter Certification Test if you think that getting certified is the next step you need to take. It would also be a good idea to talk to a few drafters to see how they got to where they are, and what advice they have about navigating your pursuit of a drafting career.

vironmental company and found my true calling. I have always been a believer in being environmentally conscious and that job offer gave me a taste of drafting. I started in environmental drafting and during the 10 years I worked there I expanded my drafting experience to include environmental, geotechnical, structural, indoor air quality, and accident reconstruction. I not only utilized the drafting skills taught to me in college but through work experience I learned about the environmental industry. After 10 years I made a decision to do what I have always wanted to do, have my own business. So after 10 years I left my job and started my own drafting company.

What are the keys to success in your career?

One thing I know about drafting is you have to love it. I lost that love for a while when I was working for my previous employer because it became a "job." Since starting my own company, the passion I once had for drafting has returned and I love drafting again. But the most important thing I can share with anyone in the drafting industry is to learn about the industry you are in. This makes the drafting much easier and makes you a more efficient drafter. When I first started in the environmental industry the engineers would draw out the groundwater contours for me then I would trace them with a digitizer. That was so much wasted time, so I sat down with one of the engineers one day and asked them to teach me how to contour drawings myself with just the data. Once I learned how, the engineers just started giving me the data and I would plot the contours myself. I truly believe that if you learn the industry you are in, you will advance your own knowledge and skills as a CADD drafter.

Find the path that's right for you. If you do not have the finances or the time to go back to school full time right now, you can still set off in that direction anyway. Online and technical courses can be applied towards a full bachelor's degree, so you can always start with those and work your way towards your eventual goal. If you do not think you are ready to take the Drafter Certification Test, then give yourself an extra year of drafting education to make sure you are adequately prepared. Once you are certified, check out the Drafting section of the Top USA Jobs Web site to find employment in your area: http://drafting.jobs.topusajobs.com.

Landmarks

If you are in your twenties . . . Even though a full bachelor's degree is not required by most employers, you might want to consider getting one. Four years of full-time school does seem tedious, but at this age you will be finished before you know it. If your life and schedule will not allow for a full four-year program, look into technical schools or community colleges. Now would also be the time to take an internship under a professional drafter. You will gain experience and make connections that will serve you well in your future profession.

If you are in your thirties or forties . . . Going back to school full time is most likely not a realistic option. There are still plenty of great two-year programs or online courses you can educate yourself with. You could be currently working in a job field that is closely related to drafting. If this is the case, you might already posses a fair amount of knowledge necessary to the field of drafting. With another design course, or some more CADD experience under your belt, you may be able to pass the Drafter Certification Test and start practicing as a drafter. Get some information on the test to find out how much more knowledge you need to acquire to become certified.

If you are in your fifties . . . Chances are you work in a visual career field and have gathered a good deal of knowledge that is applicable to drafting work. Seek out small architecture firms in your area. Though they may not be able to pay much, offering your drafting services to a freelance architect is a great way to gain some drafting experience.

If you are over sixty . . . Your years of job experience paired with visual ability and drawing skills may qualify you for drafting jobs even if you are not certified. Before seeking out drafting jobs, make sure you fill yourself in on the computer software component of drafting. It would be a good idea to take a course or a tutorial in how to use CADD software. You can find information on that here: http://www.caddprimer.com.

Further Resources

The **American Design Drafting Association Newsletter**, or ADDA, was established in 1948, and is still the premiere resource not only for drafting information, but for drafting as it relates to other fields such as engineering, digital imaging, and architecture. Signing up for their newsletter will keep you informed on the latest developments and news in drafting and related industries.   http://www.adda.org/content/view/90/85

The Drafting Zone Web site is the go-to place for up-to-date information on drafting standards, technical terms, and mechanical information. http://www.draftingzone.com

The Lazy Drafter is an easy-to-read, comprehensive blog maintained by a drafter. It offers tips, tricks and links about drafting software, not to mention funny anecdotes on the world of drafting.   http://www.lazydrafter. com

Industrial Designer

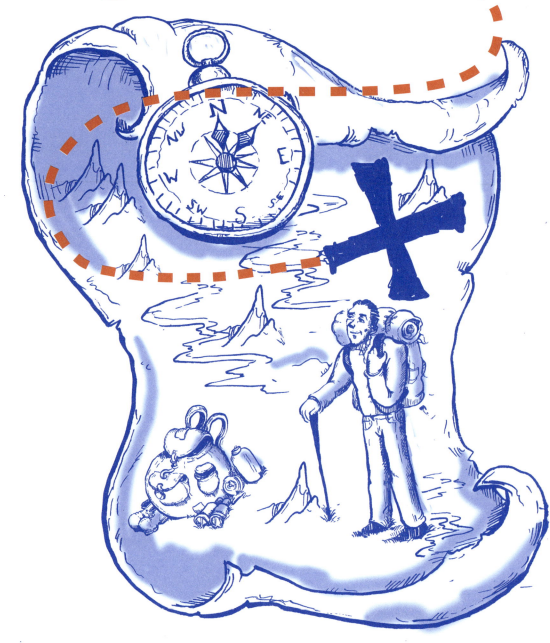

Industrial Designer

Career Compasses

Get your bearings on what it takes to become a successful industrial designer.

Caring about the field enough to keep abreast of the latest developments, in order to come up with new design concepts and ideas (40%)

Relevant Knowledge of the computer-aided industrial design system (20%)

Ability to Manage Stress in a competitive profession that requires meticulous attention to detail (20%)

Communication Skills to convey design ideas to the various professionals involved in a product's design, and the client who has hired you (20%)

Destination: Industrial Designer

The Volkswagen Beetle. The iPod. The Swiffer mop. These are products that have gained near-iconic status in our modern lives. Good advertising may be the initial reason that we decide to buy one of these things, but it is good design that makes us keep on buying them. Behind each of these successful product designs lies a successful industrial designer.

Industrial designers are responsible for every aspect of a product's design, from its function and safety to its color and style. They employ skills such as artistic abilities, engineering knowledge, and market and consumer research to prepare a design. Most industrial designers specialize in a particular type of product design. Medical tools, cars, musical equipment, and furniture are a few examples. As certain technologies become outdated, so do the products that employ them. Industrial designers are hired not only to create new design concepts but also to re-vamp existing ones. With the rapid expansion of technology, companies today are more and more seeking industrial designers who can keep their products on the cutting edge of design technology. For this reason, the mastery of computer-aided industrial design (CAID) tools is an important skill for an industrial designer to have. CAID allows for a faster, more sophisticated design process, and has become a vital part of an industrial designer's work. The field of industrial design is becoming increasingly competitive; even though the need for industrial designers is expected to grow, so is the number of those entering the job field. To stand out from the competition and increase your job prospects, it is a good idea to keep current your knowledge of the latest computer technologies.

Essential Gear

NASAD Handbook. Available in print or online, the National Association of Schools of Art and Design directory provides all the information you need in order to fulfill the educational requirements necessary to become an industrial designer. The online version is available at http://nasad.arts-accredit.org/index.jsp?page=Handbook+2009-2010.

As an industrial designer, you will work both in and outside of the office. In order to create a product design, you must first do a fair amount of research on the product. This involves reading consumer reports or talking to potential consumers, visiting trade shows or manufacturing plants, and talking to the company that will be producing the product. Once information has been gathered, the industrial designer creates a rough sketch or diagram of a design concept. A lot of times the CAID system is used during this phase of design, but not always. Some designers will draw by hand, or build a three-dimensional model of the product out of clay or wood. The industrial designer then shows the sketch or model to the company, and discusses what adjustments must be made to the initial design concept. The company's corporate strategy staff may meet with the industrial designer to make sure the product design appropriately reflects the company's image. During the latter stages of design, an industrial designer usually uses CAID to hammer out details. Finalizing a design may also involve running the product through safety tests or consumer trials, or meeting with engineers or supplies to figure out how the product can be manufactured in a more efficient and cost-effective way.

If you are an industrial designer working for a large design firm or a manufacturing establishment, you usually have fairly regular hours and health benefits. Working for a large firm also means less freedom to choose which clients or companies you design for. Freelancing or working for a small firm allows you to be more selective with your clients, but means you will need to be able to market yourself to attract work. If you freelance, you will be able to create your own work schedule; however, if the buck stops with you longer hours may be required in order to complete a design.

Artistic talent is an important characteristic to possess as an industrial designer, as it is an incredibly visual profession. Some industrial design bachelor's degree programs require you to have at least a year of art or design courses under your belt before enrolling, and some employers may require you to submit a portfolio of your work. You must possess technical knowledge and computer skills in order to navigate the CAID system and other design software. Communication skills are also important, as the job involves meeting with various other professionals to conduct research, and requires that you be able to express your design concepts clearly to a client. The most successful industrial designers are imaginative, well informed, and able to adapt to the shifts in design trends. To keep ahead of the competition, it is vital to constantly seek out new information and incorporate new ideas into your work.

Essential Gear

CAID Software. Computer-aided industrial design software is an instrumental part of modern industrial design. It allows you to draw and visualize completed designs with the click of a mouse. There are a variety of programs used in the field of industrial design, and most of them can be located here: http://www.novedge.com/Start_ID.asp.

Unlike other jobs in the engineering field, you do not have to obtain a license to work as an industrial designer. Most employers require that you possess a bachelor's degree in engineering, architecture, design, or a related field. The National Association of Schools of Art and Design Web site (http://nasad.arts-accredit.org) provides a link to purchase the directory of accredited degree programs. The NASAD Directory also provides information on two-year community colleges and online programs, so if the idea of completing a four-year degree program seems intimidating, you can ease your way into it by enrolling in one of these. Going back to school may sound tedious, but if you love design, the classes you will take while pursuing a bachelor's degree can actually be enjoyable. These classes will also put you in touch with many people in the field who may be able to help you in your future career as an industrial designer.

You Are Here

Before all else, design your path into this exciting career.

Do you have a strong background in art or design? Industrial design is a highly creative job field. Though computer-aided design systems are used, industrial designers must still possess basic drawing skills. If you are interested in entering this field, it is probably because you are an artistic person and naturally in tune with the aesthetics of the world around you. Go through any old portfolios you have to see if any of your old work would be relevant to present to degree programs or potential employers.

Are you always seeking out new ideas and information? The industrial designers who get the most work are the ones who come up with the most original design concepts. In order to be original, you must have imagination, but you must also keep constant track of the ideas that are already out there. The best industrial designers are naturally curious about the latest design concepts, and love discovering a new way to improve upon an old design.

Are you able to clearly express your creative vision to others? Many people are involved in creating a product. Many people are affected by a product's design. To become a successful industrial designer, you need to be able to communicate your vision effectively to different kinds of people. You will need to explain your design concept in terms that both the financial department of a company and the manufacturing plant workers can understand.

Navigating the Terrain

How can you become an industrial designer?

I have a bachelor's degree in a field related to industrial design

I have a bachelor's degree in an unrelated field

I do not have a bachelor's degree

Contact potential employers and assemble application pack

Get a degree in industrial design

Put together a portfolio of past art/design work

Apply for jobs at a firm or seek out freelance work

Research educational degree program

Organizing Your Expedition

Before you set out, know where you are going.

Decide on a destination. What kind of industrial design can you see yourself doing? Are you more interested in mechanics and mathematics? Then maybe industrial design work in the automobile industry would be right for you. Are you interested in finding solutions to household problems? Then a career in appliance design would be your path. It is important to visualize where you fit into the field of industrial design when charting your career course. Check out a few industrial design firm Web sites to get a feel for what kind of work, and work environment, would most suit you and your strengths and interests.

Scout the terrain. Doing some research will help you clarify and solidify your career path and goals. Contact the National Association of Schools for Art and Design. Ask someone there to give you some advice on pursuing a career in industrial design. Visit the Web site for the Industrial Designers Society of America (http://www.idsa.org) and find out if there are any informational seminars in your area. Attending these seminars can put you in touch with people who can answer any questions you have about entering the field of industrial design.

Find the path that's right for you. If you cannot go back to school full time right now, that is okay. While education in the field is a more typical path to a career in industrial design, there are other ways of getting there. For instance, many Web sites, publications, or companies offer design contests to the public. Instead of just reading about design, why not jump in and actually try it? Take a look at Yanko Design's "Submit a Design" option on its Web site, located here: http://www.yankodesign. com/tips-publication. Innovation is the name of the game in this profession, and new ideas are always valued, no matter how much or how little education someone has had.

Landmarks

If you are in your twenties . . . Chances are you are amenable to relocating. This gives you a wide range of educational options in the field of industrial design. Check out the NASAD handbook for the list of accredited degree programs and decide which ones you would like to apply to. If you have not had much experience with design, take a course or two before applying to schools, and volunteer to work for an industrial design firm in your area.

If you are in your thirties or forties . . . You probably have some experience with art or design. The skills you have been using in your current career are most likely applicable to certain aspects of industrial design. Call potential employers to find out what is missing from your qualifications. You may not need to Go back to school. Even if you do not, you will probably need to take a course or two on computer-aided industrial design. Talk to an industrial designer in your area to find out how they got to where they are, and how they recommend you acquire knowledge on the CAID system.

Notes from the Field
Arthur Carr
President and chief designer, TransForm Design
Washington, D.C.

How did you get started as an industrial designer?

I was studying architecture in school and was frustrated. One of my professors suggested that I go to a school that offers a variety of the arts including Industrial Design. I took some courses at RISD, loved the field and graduated two years later from Pratt in Brooklyn. While I was at Pratt I received a fellowship with two architects to study self-defining rigid and soft fabric structures. I fell in love with innovative portable structures. I got a job designing tents and other portable equipment. A couple years later I opened my own firm, TransForm Design.

Why did you want to get into industrial designing?

I love the quick ideation. Every day there are new challenges. I feel as if I am always doing something that has never been done before. I am always learning. I have great clients that are passionate about their products. There is nothing better than being part of a passionate team trying to make a groundbreaking product.

How did you break in?

In my first job I did whatever was needed. I spent months making instructions on rapidly deploying tents. Eventually I was designing and seeing my products used. I was hired away by another firm. I left that company as director of design and was lucky enough to continue to work with them under contract for another 10 years while working with other clients.

What are the keys to success in your career?

Listening and putting the ego in check at the right time. You need strong convictions to be a good designer, but you need to know when to put it out, when to put it in check, and to always be receptive. A design that does not meet your clients' needs is not a good design. At the same time, your client is looking to you to be the last word on design issues. Once you are totally wrapped around the requirements and issues you have to be out there, proactive, and fight for the direction that you think is important.

If you are in your fifties . . . The Industrial Designers Society of America has a great events calendar on their Web site that provides information on industrial design seminars, lectures, and conferences. Attend an event in your area and talk to a member of IDSA to find out about industrial designing volunteer opportunities, and general-entry design competitions. Take a look here: http://www.idsa.org/calendar.html.

If you are over sixty . . . Any background in the arts or related fields is a true advantage at this point. Perhaps you taught painting or sculpture at the high school or college level, or have experience with woodworking or construction. Though it may be difficult to break into the professional ranks without significant computer skills, you can still pursue design projects on a freelance basis. Think about items around your own home that you would like to see improved. Keep track of your ideas, draw out your plans, and steadily build a portfolio that you may show to potential fabricators.

Further Resources

The **Industrial Designers Society of America** maintains a Web site that is the go-to source for all things industrial design related: news, events, resources, employment opportunities, contact information, and more. http://www.idsa.org

Core77 is a cutting-edge online publication that provides not only a wealth of information on industrial design, but open discussion forums, competition information, job postings, and a store with an extensive industrial design book selection.   http://www.core77.com

Yanko Design is an international Internet meeting place for industrial design professionals and enthusiasts all over the world. http://www.yankodesign.com

Broadcast and Sound Engineering Technician

Broadcast and Sound Engineering Technician

Career Compasses

Get your bearings on what it takes to become a successful broadcast and sound engineering technician.

Relevant Knowledge of mechanical, electronic, and computer technology (40%)

Ability to Manage Stress in order to perform job duties under pressure and production deadlines (30%)

Caring about job duties enough to be willing to concentrate and focus when working overtime to troubleshoot problems (20%)

Organizational Skills to keep track of the different functions and capabilities of various kinds of electronic, mechanical and computer equipment (10%)

Destination: Broadcast and Sound Engineering Technician

When we turn on your local television station to find out about a breaking news story, we do not pay much attention to the microphone because our attention is focused on the reporter using it while they speak into the camera. Broadcast and sound engineering technicians are the people who make sure that the microphone (and the camera) are working properly. Thanks to these technicians, we can watch our nightly news program without worrying about the equipment being used to deliver it to us.

Broadcast and sound engineering technicians set up, operate, and maintain the electrical equipment used to produce TV and radio shows, films, plays, songs, and also things such as sporting events or conferences. A director or producer works with the performer using the equipment, and a broadcast and sound engineering technician works with the equipment itself, making sure it is functioning so that a production runs smoothly.

In recent years, a lot of traditional electronic equipment has been replaced by computer software, and those interested in becoming a broadcast or sound engineering technician will better their job options if they become knowledgeable about the latest developments in computer and digital technology. Since June 2009, TV stations have been required by law to use digital signals instead of analog, and although there is no law yet in the radio arena, those stations are also turning to digital broadcast signals. This change-over, plus the increasing

Essential Gear

Amateur Radio License. This is especially useful if you are interested in working as a technician in radio. Obtaining your amateur license is a great way to get started in producing, engineering, and broadcasting radio programs. More information is available here: http://www.hamuniverse.com.

popularity of technology such as cable Internet access and on-demand television, means that many new jobs will be popping up in the broadcast and sound engineering field. An employment increase of 17 percent is predicted during the next decade, which is faster than the average for other professions.

The field of broadcast and sound engineering can be broken down into a few categories. Sound engineering technicians work with the sound equipment used to record, mix, and manufacture music, vocals, and sound effects. Broadcast technicians work with equipment involved in radio or television broadcasts. As its job title suggests, audio and video equipment technicians work with audio and video equipment such as microphones, video screens, and mixing boards. Radio operators work with the equipment used in transmitting communications between stations.

Work environment for this career varies depending on what kind of technician you are. Generally, as a technician you spend your time inside, setting up, operating, and repairing equipment. However, if you work for a broadcast news station, you may spend time outside, accompanying the camera crew (and the camera) to various locations. Being employed by a large television or radio station means a 40-hour workweek, with occasional overtime to meet deadlines. Working for a smaller station means a more grueling schedule, usually more than 40 hours, and also a wider range of job duties. Just like a doctor, technicians can sometimes be "on call" even when they are not technically working, so that the station or studio can summon them in to fix any unforeseen equipment malfunctions.

Just as those interested in working as auto mechanics are interested in cars, those interested in working as a broadcast and sound engineering technicians are interested in electronic (and now digital) equipment.

Essential Gear

Vectorscope. This device is used for controlling both video and audio signals, something you will need to monitor in your work as a broadcast and sound engineering technician. Previously, vectorscopes were their own entity, but waveform monitors have begun to be manufactured with built-in vectorscope capabilities.

An important characteristic that will allow you to turn this interest into an actual career is the ability to problem solve under pressure. In order to be a successful broadcast or sound engineering technician, you must be able to stay calm and focused while working against the clock. You will find more job opportunities if you are adaptable to various environments and schedules.

Due to the pressurized nature of working to meet production deadlines, being a broadcast and sound engineering technician can be mentally stressful. Technical problems may arise at the last minute, requiring you to put in more hours than you originally anticipated. Being on call means that you must be thinking about your job even during non-working hours. Physical demands of the job can include carrying heavy equipment, climbing up poles to set-up lights or sound systems, or crouching in uncomfortable positions to repair equipment. The average yearly salary for professional sound and broadcast engineering technicians is approximately $35,000.

The good thing about becoming a broadcast or sound engineering technician is that there are not formal educational requirements, and if you have some technical knowledge under your belt, it will not be difficult to find some kind of work in the field. You can pick up a lot of the skills you need through on-the-job training at an entry-level position, and then apply to higher-paying jobs or eventually move on to freelance work. Some technicians enter the field after they have completed a year or two at a technical school, community college, or vocational program. Taking some courses in broadcast or computer technology before applying for jobs will most likely increase your employment opportunities. It will also put you in touch with people who may be valuable connections in your future job search. Another path to a career as a technician is to become certified by the Society of Broadcast Engineers. Though certification is not required for employment, it is an easy way to prove your credentials to potential employers.

You Are Here

Start here to find your way to a career as a broadcast or sound engineering technician.

Are you technologically savvy? If you are interested in becoming a broadcast or sound engineering technician, you may already be working with computers in your current career. Even if you are not, you have probably already picked up skills from using computers in your free time that will prove to be valuable in this job field. Check out the Society of Broadcast Engineers Web site to find books that can educate you on the latest technological developments in the field: http://www.sbe.org/edu_books.php.

Do you enjoy problem solving? When your car gets a flat tire, do you attempt to fix it yourself or do you call roadside assistance? If you would definitely opt to fix the tire yourself, you are the type of person who would make a good broadcast and sound engineering technician. For those who enjoy their work in this job field, unexpected problems are a satisfying challenge as opposed to a cause for alarm.

Are you adaptable when confronted with different people and places? Your work as a broadcast and sound engineering technician may be stressful, but it is never boring. In a traditional office job, you

Navigating the Terrain

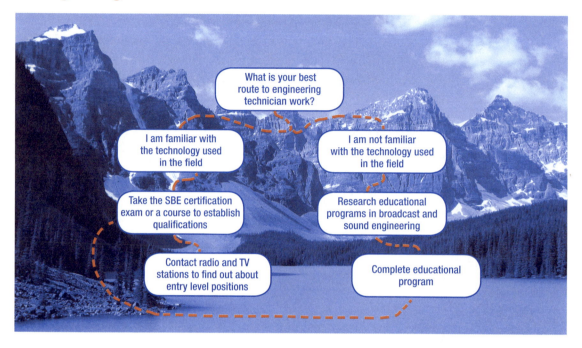

report to the same desk and the same coworkers every day. In this job, the setting and people you work with are constantly changing. It is very important to be able to adapt to new surroundings, and to make a good impression on the various people you work with. If your employers like you and find you easy to work with, they will hire you for more work, or recommend you to other employers.

Organizing Your Expedition

Before you set out, know where you are going.

Decide on a destination. Think about your strengths and interests to decide what kind of technician you want to be. If you are more interested in working with visuals, then becoming a broadcast technician or a video equipment technician is the appropriate career field for you. If your interests lie more on the aural side, then you will most likely be pursuing a career as a sound engineering technician, audio equipment technician, or a radio operator.

Scout the terrain. Once you have pinpointed what kind of technician you would like to become, it is time to figure out where you would like to work. If you live in a more rural area, pay a visit to your local television or radio station and talk to someone there about possible entry-level employment opportunities. If you live in a larger city, you might need to contact several different stations of varying sizes to find out which ones would be most likely to hire you. If you need to take a year of education before applying to jobs, then look into vocational school or community colleges. Talk to potential employers or working technicians to get recommendations for programs in your area, or online.

Find the path that's right for you. If being thrown into broadcast news at a large station seems intimidating right now, then apply for smaller, less pressurized positions. You can always work your way up to your eventual career goals by starting small. It is a good idea to gather experience and sharpen your skills as a technician on a smaller scale, so that when you advance to a larger position (and salary) you are prepared and can make a good impression with your employers immediately.

Landmarks

If you are in your twenties . . . Enrolling in a degree or certification program in the broadcast and engineering field is always an option. You are probably amenable to relocation at this stage in your life, which is an advantage in getting hired immediately. As long as you have some technical knowledge and are willing to work odd hours, smaller stations or studios in rural areas will hire you even if you have no formal job experience. If you are willing to relocate for a year or so to wherever there is a job opening, you will be able to gain valuable job experience, and perhaps a more impressive job title to put on your résumé.

If you are in your thirties or forties . . . Although you have been working in different career field, you are probably interested in becoming a broadcast or sound engineering technician because you have attempted

Notes from the Field

Tim Pearce
System designer, Acentech
Trevose, Pennyslvania

How did you get started in the field of broadcast/sound engineering?

Like many in our industry, it began with an interest in music and a fascination with technology. This led me into technical theater, music recording, and television production in college. I also had a definite inclination towards math and science. At the time, there were few university programs focusing on audio, so I chose to study electrical engineering with the knowledge that ultimately I wanted a career in this field, even if I did not know exactly what that might mean.

Why did you want to get into broadcast/sound engineering?

It started with a decision not to pursue a career as a musician, but to still be involved in the process from a more technical side. That is not to say there is not a component of art in what we do; in fact, it is the mix of technical versus artistic elements that appeals to many people. I also saw it as a way to experience the results of my design efforts, something many engineers never get to do.

How did you break in?

I was able to find opportunities through a combination of practical experience (volunteering at the college TV studio, running sound freelance for bar bands, hauling equipment into and out of theaters) and an undergraduate degree in engineering.

What are the keys to success in your career?

No two career paths are identical, but I think one important element was to keep my education general, and learn the specifics of the industry through experience. I have always thought of an engineering education as vocational in nature, but broad enough to qualify one for any number of fields. The other key has been continued interest in current technology and how it can be utilized to advance the industry.

some amateur technician work in the past. You have most likely picked up skills that you will be able to use when dealing with equipment such as microphones and mixing equipment. At this point it would be a good idea to take a computer course or two to update yourself on the latest advancements in digital and computer technology. Talk to someone at your local television or radio station, or research informational seminars in your area at the Society of Broadcast Engineers Web site. Find out how much, if any, education you need to complete before applying for jobs.

If you are in your fifties . . . If you enjoy working with mechanical equipment, your services (and experience) will be valuable to your local television or radio station. Go there in person to inquire about paid odd jobs or volunteer opportunities as a technician. With your life experience, they may even offer you a job training younger technicians. Consider taking a course on computer and digital technology, perhaps from an online program such as ITT Technical Institute (http://itt-tech.edu).

If you are over sixty . . . Seek out local-access television stations in your area and apply for volunteer opportunities. Even if you have little or no technical expertise, producers at these local stations will help train new volunteers in all areas of television production, including sound engineering.

Further Resources

The **Society of Broadcast Engineers** is the only organization of its kind, and its Web site provides career information and helpful links for people with all levels of experience in the field of broadcast engineering. http://www.sbe.org

Entertainment Engineering magazine is the premiere publication for the latest news and technological developments in the field of technical engineering as it pertains to the entertainment industry. http://www.entertainmentengineering.com

Media Arts School Guide is an extensive and easy-to-navigate Web site that offers information and advice on all different kinds of degree and certification programs in all fields related to media arts. If you are searching for courses in broadcast and sound engineering, this is a great resource. http://www.collegebound.net/media-arts-school-guide

Industrial Production Manager

Industrial Production Manager

Career Compasses

Get your bearings on what it takes to become a successful industrial production manager.

Ability to Manage Stress in a job field that requires peak performance during long hours and pressurized situations (30%)

Relevant Knowledge of the statistics, mechanics, and technology involved in the manufacturing process (25%)

Organizational Skills to keep track of the many different facets of production (25%)

Communication Skills to effectively relay information and ideas to different professionals and workers involved in production (20%)

Destination: Industrial Production Manager

Our modern lives are full of stuff. Some stuff we use for transportation purposes, like cars. Some stuff we use for nourishment purposes, like utensils. Some stuff we use for recreational purposes, like televisions. Although "stuff" is one way of defining it, *manufactured goods* is a more technical term for it. All goods are manufactured by a series of coordinated production activities at a manufacturing plant. The person responsible for the coordination and management of these activities is called an industrial production manager. It is the responsibility of the industrial production manager to make sure that a manufactured good is produced up to quality standards in a timely, efficient, and cost-effective manner. Industrial production managers coordinate the many different aspects of the manufacturing process by meeting with and relaying information to the various other professionals involved in production, and the company that will end up selling the good.

In the past, goods were manufactured by a mass assembly line, with many workers performing one particular task over and over again. In recent years, "lean" production, or team product assembly, has replaced the traditional methods. These changes, plus advancements that have been made in quality control programs and computer software, have allowed corporations to eliminate much of the "support staff" involved in the manufacturing process. Thus a slight decline in overall production employment is predicted over the course of the next decade. However, because much of the job involves in-person supervising, trouble-shooting, and decision-making, the industrial production manager position will remain a necessity in the manufacturing and production of goods.

Outside of the office, your job duties as an industrial production manager include overseeing production activities and inspecting machinery at the manufacturing plant, training staff, and meeting with various other professionals such as financial departments heads of sales or supplies. While industrial production managing is not strictly an office job, part of your time is spent in an office. There, you perform tasks such as reviewing cost estimates, coming up

Essential Gear

Statistics. Industrial production managers are well versed in the facts, figures, and data that apply to their field. Find all the basic information you need (and then some) in the Online Statistics Textbook: http://www.statsoft.com/textbook/stathome.html.

with ways to improve manufacturing techniques, or reviewing product data. Many production facilities continue manufacturing operations 24 hours a day, and for this reason, most industrial production managers work fairly long hours—often more than 50 per week. When deadlines must be met and something goes wrong at the manufacturing plant, you are expected to report to work no matter what time it is, and stay there until you have come up with a solution for the problem at hand.

Rising to meet a challenge when the going gets tough is an important quality to have as an industrial production manager. It is your responsibility to oversee many different branches of the production process, and you must possess both organizational and communication skills to make sure not only that *you* perform well under pressure, but that others do too. You also must be naturally inquisitive and willing to keep learning about new technologies. Employers will be more likely to hire you if they see that you are continually searching for better, more efficient production techniques.

Essential Gear

APICS Dictionary. Just like in any job field, if you want to become a successful industrial production manager you have to know the lingo. The Association for Operation Management Dictionary is available online at http://www.apics.org, as well as in book form.

Industrial production managing can be a satisfying job if you are suited to it. Still, due to the long, unusual hours, and the fact that you must often be "on call" in case an emergency situation arises, the job can also prove incredibly stressful no matter how much you love the work. You may be called in the middle of the night to deal with an equipment malfunction at the manufacturing plant, and then have to attend meetings or deliver reports the next day on very little sleep. The amount of responsibility involved in industrial production managing has increased over the years, in that there are more people under your supervision. This means that if something goes wrong, a client or company can hold you accountable for any mistakes made. The good news about entering a pressurized field like this is that the pay can be very good. While the average industrial production manager earns anywhere from $59,600 to $100,800, the top 10 percent of industrial production managers earn more than $130,600.

Though your chances of getting hired as an industrial production manager will be greater if you possess a bachelor's degree, there are no official educational requirements for the job position. Attitude, persistence, and performance are just as important as educational experience. Some people enter the field as production workers, and then after gaining some experience and proving themselves capable, progress up to a management position. You can also pursue a degree while working your way up. If you have a bachelor's degree in a business administration or industrial technology, you will have an easy time finding a job, though some employers will hire you to the position even if your bachelor's degree is in an unrelated field. While it is not required, becoming certified is another way to prove your credentials and abilities to potential employers. The American Society For Quality and the Association for Operations Management both offer certification programs.

You Are Here

Industrial production managers should possess natural leadership skills.

Do you have a background in management? Just like any management position, industrial production managers have to be comfortable with responsibility and confident decision-making. An entire staff is depending on your guidance to ensure that things run smoothly. If you have ever worked as a restaurant manager or held a supervisor position in retail or guest services, then you have already been employing some of the skills you would use as an industrial production manager.

Do you enjoy problem solving? Successful industrial production managers are inherently prepared for a problem. When one occurs, they are able to remain calm and focused while they solve it. Though the job can be stressful, industrial production managers who love their work find satisfaction in working toward and finding solutions to difficult situations. They must be level-headed, pragmatic, and creative in their approach, all while keeping up the morale of their staff.

Are you personable and do you work well with others? Industrial production management is an interpersonal career field. You are constantly engaging in discussions with others, and relaying information or instruction to the various people involved in the manufacturing process. Communication skills as well as a tolerance for varying points of view are necessary components of an industrial production manager's job. He or she is accountable to supervisors and responsible for staff, and may have to negotiate the needs of both.

Navigating the Terrain

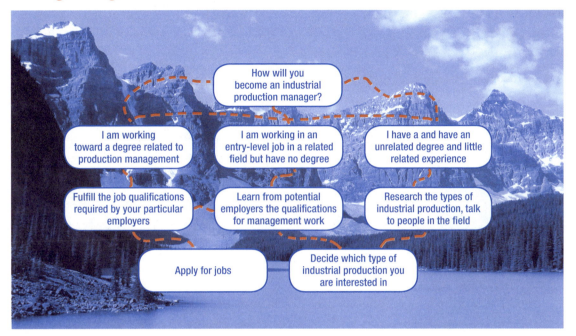

How will you become an industrial production manager?

I am working toward a degree related to production management

I am working in an entry-level job in a related field but have no degree

I have a and have an unrelated degree and little related experience

Fulfill the job qualifications required by your particular employers

Learn from potential employers the qualifications for management work

Research the types of industrial production, talk to people in the field

Apply for jobs

Decide which type of industrial production you are interested in

Organizing Your Expedition

Before you set out, know where you are going.

Decide on a destination. Can you see yourself overseeing operations at a small manufacturing plant? Or are you more interested in working as a more specialized supervisor in a branch at a larger plant? Does it matter to you what kind of goods you are involved in producing, or would you be happy to work manufacturing a variety of goods? Before you apply to industrial production management positions, or enroll in a degree program, take some time to think about your eventual career goals, and the environment you would feel most comfortable working in. Also think carefully about your existing skills: are you a natural leader, or are you more productive working as a member of a democratic team?

Scout the terrain. Find out what kind of employment opportunities there are in your area. A lot of cities specialize in a certain type of pro-

Notes from the Field

James Gabriel
Project production manager, Design Communications Ltd
Boston, Massachusetts

How did you get started as an industrial production manager?

I studied engineering in college and have a technical background. I started out doing work in project development, putting potential projects together and performing profit feasibility studies, drafting proposals, and submitting bids. Through this I grew my understanding of what is involved in a production project and evolved into a manager.

Why did you want to get into industrial production management?

I enjoy a fast-paced work environment with numerous tasks to manage and always being busy. I have always been good at time management along with the ability to delegate tasks properly.

How did you break in?

I broke in through working in project development. As I developed potential projects and projects became reality to within a few percentage points of my estimated profit margin, I was given the opportunity to try my hand in management of projects as production took place.

What are the keys to success in your career?

Having a creative mind and being able to capitalize on non-conventional solutions to problems. Having a wide array of knowledge in different materials and manufacturing processes and being able to understand which will work by only looking at conceptual renderings of a product. Time management and the ability to keep a watchful eye on the overall project as production is taking place in small parts. The ability to delegate work while having a sense of team members' strengths/weaknesses.

duction. For instance, Pittsburgh is known for its steel production, Detroit for automobile manufacturing. Familiarize yourself with any local industry, perhaps taking introductory classes in disciplines related to that industry. If you seek work in a steel refinery, for example, a geology course would prove especially beneficial. As an industrial production manager you will be called upon to know all facets of production—even those that occur before the product enters and after the product leaves the plant.

Find the path that's right for you. Consider your personality, learning preferences, and existing schedule and finances to figure out which path to your career goals is right for you. If you are new to the field, you will probably need to go back to school or enroll in a technical or vocational program to pick up the skills you will need for the job. You may want to start working at an entry-level position first and pursue your education simultaneously. If you are already working an entry-level position at a manufacturing plant and are interested in moving up, talk to your superiors about what kind of requirements you will need to fulfill, or what type of job performance they are looking for in order to promote you. Be humble, diligent, and determined.

Landmarks

If you are in your twenties . . . At this point in your life, your schedule is most likely quite flexible. It would be a good idea to look into degree or educational programs in the field of industrial production management. Though you may be able to find work without a degree, you will be able to start at a higher level (and a higher salary) with one. Contact the Association for Operations Management at their "Advancing Productivity, Innovation, and Competitive Success" Web site, located at http://www.apics.org, to find out what degree programs they recommend.

If you are in your thirties or forties . . . You have probably gathered a fair amount of work experience and skills that can be applied to a career in industrial production management. You should contact potential employers to find out how much more, if any, knowledge and education you need to acquire to find jobs in the field. Check out the Association for Operations Management's online seminar series. Find one that is most appropriate to your career goals.

If you are in your fifties . . . Your career and life experience can be valuable to production management, either on a professional or volunteer level. It would be a good idea to attend a career workshop in your area and talk to working industrial production managers and find out what path they took to get to where they are, and find out what kind of job opportunities are available in your area.

If you are over sixty . . . It may be difficult to transfer from another career directly into a leadership position such as industrial production manager. However, by proving that you have built up experience in a given industry you may be able to find work as a consultant to managerial staff. In this capacity you will advise, help managers solve problems, and recommend new approaches to production.

Further Resources

The **American Society for Quality** can answer all of your questions about how to pursue (and succeed at) a career in industrial production management. They have local chapters all across the country.
http://www.asq.org/sections/find.html

Quality Progress magazine provides the latest, most cutting-edge developments in the field of all areas of production management. It is available either online or in print.   http://www.asq.org/qualityprogress/index.html

Industrial Engineer

Industrial Engineer

Career Compasses

Get your bearings on what it takes to become a successful industrial engineer.

Relevant Knowledge of software, product data, and manufacturing techniques (30%)

Ability to Manage Stress in a pressurized work environment (25%)

Mathematical Skills in order to make the calculations necessary in formulating a manufacturing plan (25%)

Communication Skills to relay information to the wide variety of people involved in the manufacturing process (20%)

Destination: Industrial Engineer

Go into any store to buy something and you will see shelves full of products with the same measurements, colors, and materials. Mass-produced products with identical designs are the result of well thought-out manufacturing plans. The people who come up with these plans are called industrial engineers. To develop and plan these various systems, industrial engineers employ mathematic and scientific principles, and knowledge of factors such as market research, business organization methods, or technological methods.

Industrial engineers are hired not only to develop and implement new manufacturing systems, but to upgrade existing ones as well. This bodes well for employment opportunities in the field. In recent years manufacturing plants have increased their need for industrial engineers who can replace outdated design and production systems with newer, more efficient ones. In the coming decade, the field of industrial engineering is expected to have an employment growth of 11 percent. Still, the field remains a competitive one, and those interested in entering it should be well-informed on the latest developments in production techniques. This is especially true as manufacturing companies become more and more dependent on computer systems that can operate without a lot of "support staff."

The field of industrial engineering can be broken down into several different specializations. Industrial engineers who work in project management create production methods for specific projects; their job duties include organizing work schedules, putting together production teams, figuring out facility layout and activity, and analyzing project resources. Industrial engineers who work in supply chain management deal mainly with supplier-company relations. Strategic planning engineers are concerned with long-term projects and make long-range production plans. Ergonomics engineers deal with all human factors involved in the manufacturing process, such as worker injuries and manufactur-

Essential Gear

Computer software. These days, industrial engineers use many different kinds of computer programs in order to calculate data or simulate production techniques. GlobalSpec is an extensive software search engine that provides access to many different software programs, such as Plant Management, Work Study, and Electronic Design Animation software just to name a few: http://www.globalspec.com/ProductFinder/Industrial_Engineering_Software.

ing codes. Quality measurement and improvement engineers work with designers to improve the quality of a product or service. Financial engineering deals with the monetary side of production and cost-benefit analysis. Finally, some industrial engineers who specialize in "management of change" are called in when a company or product needs a major overhaul in its manufacturing methods.

Job duties of various industrial engineers vary. You will spend time in an office studying product data, calculating cost estimates, or testing the functionality of a production method using computerized design models. You will also spend time meeting with company executives to ensure the manufacturing methods you have come up with are fulfilling production requirements. Some time is devoted to visiting manufacturing plants to see that things are running smoothly, that people are able to work efficiently, and to take note of any adjustments need to be made. With all of this, overtime is not uncommon.

Essential Gear

Review for the Professional Engineers Examination in Industrial Engineering. In order to become a professional industrial engineer, you have to pass the engineering exams, which are eight hours long and consist mainly of multiple-choice questions. Get a head start on the exams by getting your hands on a study guide such as this one, available at major bookstores and also on Amazon.com.

As an industrial engineer you must be creative and confident in your decision-making abilities, but also willing to take suggestions from others. Sometimes a company will have a product specification that you do not agree with, so you have to be willing to compromise. You must also be organized and good at solving problems under pressure, as production plans may need to be adjusted at the last minute if things are not running efficiently. Another important quality in a successful industrial engineer is the ability to communicate with a variety of people. You need to be able to clearly express you ideas and instructions to both the executives in suits and the production workers on the assembly line.

Industrial engineering can be physically stressful when the hours get long, and you are required to work late to figure out a manufacturing issue. When meeting a production deadline, you may sometimes be required to stay late, arrive early, and perform your job duties on very little sleep. Dealing with the demands of many different people means that the job tends to be mentally stressful as well. A company might make a manufacturing request that will send production workers into overtime hours. Some companies are not in touch with the welfare of the production workers, or the capabilities of the manufacturing equipment, and can be unreasonable if you suggest an alternate method of production. Some workers and other professionals involved in production can become frustrated if new production methods are implemented at the last minute. It is up to you as an industrial engineer to create manufacturing systems and management methods that will satisfy everyone's needs, and this can be a tricky, exhausting task. The upside to working in a stressful job field is that the pay is fairly good. Industrial engineers can make anywhere from $50,000 to more than $100,000 a year.

Possessing an engineering license is a fairly standard requirement in finding work as a professional in the field. Licensed engineers are known as P.E.'s, or Professional Engineers, and becoming one will widen your job opportunities as well as increase your chances at a bigger salary. Obtaining your industrial engineering license means passing the Fundamentals of Engineering exam and the Principles of Engineering Exam. The application requirements for these exams vary from state to state. Some states will not allow you to take the exams unless you have a degree in engineering, some allow you to apply with a degree in an unrelated field, and a few will let you take the exams even if you do not have a bachelor's degree but have completed a certification program or have a fair amount of work experience in the field. Some engineers gain experience through production work or other manufacturing positions while they pursue a degree in engineering, or take courses to prepare for the licensure exams. As it is in any challenging job field, you can start at an entry-level position and work your way toward your eventual career goals. The important thing is to be persistent, and prove to your employers that while you may not be licensed yet, you have what it takes to become a professional industrial engineer.

You Are Here

Rig up the infrastructure you will need to enter a career as an industrial engineer.

Do you have strength in mathematics? Any kind of engineering involves math. Industrial engineers are constantly calculating product and manufacturing data in order to come up with newer, faster methods of production. If you are interested in becoming an industrial engineer, math is probably one of your strengths, and measuring the world around you comes naturally. Even if you employ your math skills in your current career, it would be a good idea to talk to a working industrial engineer to find out what kind of mathematics they use on a daily basis. If your skills are rusty, it might be helpful to take a refresher math course even before you enroll in an engineering program.

Are you an analytical person who enjoys problem solving? Industrial engineers are problem solvers. If something goes wrong, they rise to the challenge of analyzing the issue and finding a solution. Industrial engineers are inherently prepared for bumps along the way, and constantly looking around and absorbing new ideas that may help with an old problem. If you find satisfaction from working through a difficult situation, then you will find satisfaction as an industrial engineer.

Are you personable and do you have good communication skills? There are many different people involved in the manufacturing process—executives, scientists, assembly line workers—and the industrial engineer must take all of these people into account when creating a manufacturing plan. It is not a solitary field, and in order to find job success and satisfaction, you must work well as part of a team.

Navigating the Terrain

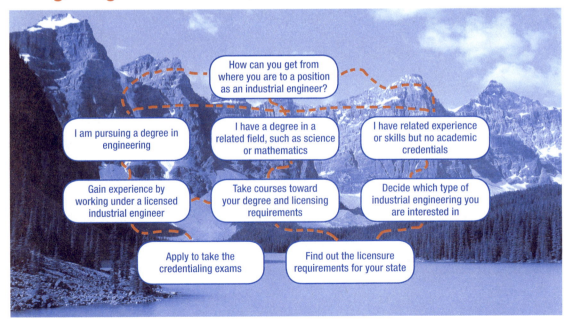

How can you get from where you are to a position as an industrial engineer?

I am pursuing a degree in engineering

I have a degree in a related field, such as science or mathematics

I have related experience or skills but no academic credentials

Gain experience by working under a licensed industrial engineer

Take courses toward your degree and licensing requirements

Decide which type of industrial engineering you are interested in

Apply to take the credentialing exams

Find out the licensure requirements for your state

Organizing Your Expedition

Before you set out, know where you are going.

Decide on a destination. Consider your strengths and interests and decide what sort of industrial engineering you can see yourself doing. If you are good with numbers and finances, you may be suited to financial engineering. If you are interested in cars, you probably will be pursuing industrial engineering jobs that specialize in automobile production. While it's possible to obtain a degree in generalized engineering, you'll make your path to career success much easier if you have a more specific idea of where you fit into the field.

Scout the terrain. Do some research. Find out what your state's application requirements are for the licensure exams. What kind of a degree to you need? If you already have some academic credentials under your belt, find out from the American Society for Engineering Education if they will count towards an engineering degree (http://www.asee.org/). Contact the manufacturing plants or design companies in your area and find out what qualifications they require for hiring, and if they offer any internships or volunteer opportunities for someone who is starting out in the field. Go to the Web site for the Institute for Industrial Engineers to find out about industrial engineering seminars in your area (http://www.iienet2.org/Default.aspx). Attending a seminar or conference will allow you to meet professionals in the field. Go to a conference prepared with specific questions about how to pursue a career in industrial engineering. If people see that you are appreciative and enthusiastic, and that you have done some prior research, they will be happy to answer your questions, point you in the right direction, and may even be potential future contacts.

Find the path that's right for you. Employers and professional contacts will be more likely to respond to a job application if you (and your résumé) are able to present a clearly-defined idea of exactly who you are and what you can offer. Figure out a way to make yourself stand out. What are you really good at? Strategizing? Money management? Re-imagining old ideas? Be both realistic and specific when considering your strengths and

Notes from the Field
Karen Bangs
Director of the women's engineering program and lecturer
of industrial and manufacturing engineering, California
Polytechnic State University, San Luis Obispo
San Luis Obispo, California

How did you get started as an industrial engineer?

My first job was in the semiconductor industry managing capital projects for the wafer fabrication operation.

Why did you want to get into industrial engineering?

I actually started studying as a mechanical engineer but realized I did not like that field. A friend told me about industrial engineering, that it had more of a business aspect to it.

How did you break in?

My coworkers were very helpful and I asked a lot of questions. The training was on-the-job. Much like just about any job I have had in the field: operations finance, supply chain management, and now university professor.

What are the keys to success in your career?

Hard work! Be willing to take chances. Be willing to take on responsibilities outside of your direct job scope. Find a mentor or coach in your company to work with. Learn and practice good communication skills. Take initiative and be willing to go that extra mile.

weaknesses. Be specific in your pursuit of work experience and academic credentials, so you can build a résumé that shows exactly where you fit in to the field of industrial engineering.

Landmarks

If you are in your twenties . . . If you do not have an engineering degree, now is the time to go back to school and get one. This may seem like a daunting task, so it is important to get inspired before you take the educational plunge. If you have cold feet or feel unsure about your career goals, take a few engineering courses at a community college to interact with people who have similar goals. If you do not know where to start, visit the Web site for the American Society for Engineering Education (http://www.asee.org) for a list of schools and educational advice.

If you are in your thirties or forties . . . You most likely have acquired some job experience that is relevant to the field of industrial engineering, and that is a valuable qualification. Your schedule may not permit you to go back to school full time, but with your job experience, completing a two-year program at a technical institute, community college, or online program may qualify you to take your state's licensure exam. You may be able to find work at an entry-level production position and work your way up. Contact someone from your local chapter of the Institute of Industrial Engineers and find out what recommendations they have for you based on your current career experience. The institute also offers a series of online seminars that provide more information about various facets of the field. Go to their Web site (http://www.iienet2.org) and check out a Web seminar or two.

If you are in your fifties . . . Even though you may not possess an engineering license, you most likely possess a large amount of work experience, knowledge, and skills relevant to the field of industrial engineering. Getting licensed means working under the title of professional engineer, but even without a license, you will be able to find some kind of work in the field. Check out Industrialengineer.com to find out if there are any job opportunities in your area that you might be qualified for. Find out if the Institute of Industrial Engineers is holding any informational seminars or conferences in your area.

If you are over sixty . . . As long as you are willing to keep an open mind and learn from people younger than you, then your career and life experience will prove useful in the field of industrial engineering. Look into volunteering opportunities. Nonprofits such as Engineers Without Borders (http://www.ewbnewyork.com) are good places to find volunteer work.

Further Resources

The **Institute of Industrial Engineers** Web site contains an extensive database of information, news, employment links, helpful contacts and more. Also found here is the online version of *Industrial Engineer* magazine, the premier publication of the field.   http://www.iienet2.org

Industrial Engineer.com is a career-oriented site, described as "the place to showcase industrial engineering jobs and products to industrial engineers."   http://www.industrialengineer.com

Appendix A

Going Solo: Starting Your Own Business

Starting your own business can be very rewarding—not only in terms of potential financial success, but also in the pleasure derived from building something from the ground up, contributing to the community, being your own boss, and feeling reasonably in control of your fate. However, business ownership carries its own obligations—both in terms of long hours of hard work and new financial and legal responsibilities. If you succeed in growing your business, your responsibilities only increase. Many new business owners come in expecting freedom only to find themselves chained tighter to their desks than ever before. Still, many business owners find greater satisfaction in their career paths than do workers employed by others.

The Internet has also changed the playing field for small business owners, making it easier than ever before to strike out on your own. While small mom-and-pop businesses such as hairdressers and grocery stores have always been part of the economic landscape, the Internet has made reaching and marketing to a niche easier and more profitable. This has made possible a boom in *microbusinesses*. Generally, a microbusiness is considered to have under ten employees. A microbusiness is also sometimes called a *SOHO* for "small office/home office."

The following appendix is intended to explain, in general terms, the steps in launching a small business, no matter whether it is selling your Web-design services or opening a pizzeria with business partners. It will also point out some of the things you will need to bear in mind. Remember also that the particular obligations of your municipality, state, province, or country may vary, and that this is by no means a substitute for doing your own legwork. Further suggested reading is listed at the end.

Crafting a Business Plan

It has often been said that success is 1 percent inspiration and 99 percent perspiration. However, the interface between the two can often be hard to achieve. The first step to taking your idea and making it reality is constructing a viable *business plan*. The purpose of a business plan is to think things all the way through, to make sure your ideas really are profitable, and to figure out the "who, what, when, where, why, and how" of your business. It fills in the details for three areas: your goals, why you think they are attainable, and how you plan to get to there. "You need to know where you're going before you take that first step," says Drew Curtis, successful Internet entrepreneur and founder of the popular newsfilter Fark.com.

Take care in writing your business plan. Generally, these documents contain several parts: An *executive summary* stating the essence of the plan; a *market summary* explaining how a need exists for the product and service you will supply and giving an idea of potential profitability by comparing your business to similar organizations; a *company description* which includes your products and services, why you think your organization will succeed, and any special advantages you have, as well as a description of *organization* and *management*; and your *marketing and sales strategy*. This last item should include market highlights and demographic information and trends that relate to your proposal. Also include a *funding request* for the amount of start-up capital you will need. This is supported by a section on *financials*, or the sort of cash flow you can expect, based on market analysis, projection, and comparison with existing companies. Other needed information, such as personal financial history, résumés, legal documents, or pictures of your product, can be placed in *appendices*.

Use your business plan to get an idea of how much startup money is necessary and to discipline your thinking and challenge your preconceived notions before you develop your cash flow. The business plan will tell you how long it will take before you turn a profit, which in turn is linked to how long it will before you will be able to pay back investors or a bank loan—which is something that anyone supplying you with money will want to know. Even if you are planning to subsist on grants or you are not planning on investment or even starting a for-profit company, the discipline imposed by the business plan is still the first step to organizing your venture.

A business plan also gives you a realistic view of your personal financial obligations. How long can you afford to live without regular income? How are you going to afford medical insurance? When will your business begin turning a profit? How much of a profit? Will you need to reinvest your profits in the business, or can you begin living off of them? Proper planning is key to success in any venture.

A final note on business plans: Take into account realistic expected profit minus realistic costs. Many small business owners begin by underestimating start-ups and variable costs (such as electricity bills), and then underpricing their product. This effectively paints them into a corner from which it is hard to make a profit. Allow for realistic market conditions on both the supply and the demand side.

Partnering Up

You should think long and hard about the decision to go into business with a partner (or partners). Whereas other people can bring needed capital, expertise, and labor to a business, they can also be liabilities. The questions you need to ask yourself are:

☞ Will this person be a full and equal partner? In other words, are they able to carry their own weight? Make a full and fair assessment of your potential partner's personality. Going into business with someone who lacks a work ethic, or prefers giving directions to working in the trenches, can be a frustrating experience.

☞ What will they contribute to the business? For instance, a partner may bring in start-up money, facilities, or equipment. However, consider if this is enough of a reason to bring them on board. You may be able to get the same advantages in another way—for instance, renting a garage rather than working out of your partner's. Likewise, doubling skill sets does not always double productivity.

☞ Do they have any liabilities? For instance, if your prospective partner has declared bankruptcy in the past, this can hurt your collective venture's ability to get credit.

☞ Will the profits be able to sustain all the partners? Many start-up ventures do not turn profits immediately, and what little they do produce can be spread thin amongst many partners. Carefully work out the math.

Also bear in mind that going into business together can put a strain on even the best personal relationships. No matter whether it is family, friends, or strangers, keep everything very professional with written agreements regarding these investments. Get everything in writing, and be clear where obligations begin and end. "It's important to go into business with the right people," says Curtis. "If you don't—if it degrades into infighting and petty bickering—it can really go south quickly."

Incorporating. . . or Not

Think long and hard about incorporating. Starting a business often requires a fairly large—and risky—financial investment, which in turn exposes you to personal liability. Furthermore, as your business grows, so does your risk. Incorporating can help you shield yourself from this liability. However, it also has disadvantages.

To begin with, incorporating is not necessary for conducting professional transactions such as obtaining bank accounts and credit. You can do this as a sole proprietor, partnership, or simply by filing a DBA ("doing business as") statement with your local court (also known as "trading as" or an "assumed business name"). The DBA is an accounting entity that facilitates commerce and keeps your business' money separate from your own. However, the DBA does not shield you from responsibility if your business fails. It is entirely possible to ruin your credit, lose your house, and have your other assets seized in the unfortunate event of bankruptcy.

The purpose of incorporating is to shield yourself from personal financial liability. In case the worst happens, only the business' assets can be taken. However, this is not always the best solution. Check your local laws: Many states have laws that prevent a creditor from seizing a non-incorporated small business' assets in case of owner bankruptcy. If you are a corporation, however, the things you use to do business that are owned by the corporation—your office equipment, computers, restaurant refrigerators, and other essential equipment—may be seized by creditors, leaving you no way to work yourself out of debt. This is why it is imperative to consult with a lawyer.

There are other areas in which being a corporation can be an advantage, such as business insurance. Depending on your business needs, insurance can be for a variety of things: malpractice, against delivery failures or spoilage, or liability against defective products or accidents. Furthermore, it is easier to hire employees, obtain credit, and buy health insurance as an organization than as an individual. However, on the downside, corporations are subject to specific and strict laws concerning management and ownership. Again, you should consult with a knowledgeable legal expert.

Among the things you should discuss with your legal expert are the advantages and disadvantages of incorporating in your jurisdiction and which type of incorporation is best for you. The laws on liability and how much of your profit will be taken away in taxes vary widely by state and country. Generally, most small businesses owners opt for *limited liability companies* (LLCs), which gives them more control and a more flexible management structure. (Another possibility is a *limited liability partnership*, or *LLP*, which is especially useful for professionals such as doctors and lawyers.) Finally, there is the *corporation*, which is characterized by transferable ownerships shares, perpetual succession, and, of course, limited liability.

Most small businesses are sole proprietorships, partnerships, or privately-owned corporations. In the past, not many incorporated, since it was necessary to have multiple owners to start a corporation. However, this is changing, since it is now possible in many states for an individual to form a corporation. Note also that the form your business takes is usually not set in stone: A sole proprietorship or partnership can switch to become an LLC as it grows and the risks increase; furthermore, a successful LLC can raise capital by changing its structure to become a corporation and selling stock.

Legal Issues

Many other legal issues besides incorporating (or not) need to be addressed before you start your business. It is impossible to speak directly to every possible business need in this brief appendix, since regulations, licenses, and health and safety codes vary by industry and locality. A restaurant in Manhattan, for instance, has to deal not only with the usual issues such as health inspectors, and the state liquor board, but obscure regulations such as New York City's cabaret laws, which prohibit dancing without a license in a place where alcohol is sold. An asbestos-abatement company, on the other hand, has a very different set of standards it has to abide by, including federal regulations. Researching applicable laws is part of starting up any business.

Part of being a wise business owner is knowing when you need help. There is software available for things like bookkeeping, business plans, and Web site creation, but generally, consulting with a knowledgeable professional—an accountant or a lawyer (or both)—is the smartest move. One of the most common mistakes is believing that just because you have expertise in the technical aspects of a certain field, you know all about running a business in that field. Whereas some people may balk at the expense, by suggesting the best way to deal with possible problems, as well as cutting through red tape and seeing possible pitfalls that you may not even have been aware of, such professionals usually more than make up for their cost. After all, they have far more experience at this than does a first-time business owner!

Financial

Another necessary first step in starting a business is obtaining a bank account. However, having the account is not as important as what you do with it. One of the most common problems with small businesses is undercapitalization—especially in brick-and-mortar businesses that sell or make something, rather than service-based businesses. The rule of thumb is that you should have access to money equal to your first year's anticipated profits, plus start-up expenses. (Note that this is not the same as having the money on hand—see the discussion on lines of credit, below.) For instance, if your annual rent, salaries, and equipment will cost $50,000 and you expect $25,000 worth of profit in your first year, you should have access to $75,000 worth of financing.

You need to decide what sort of financing you will need. Small business loans have both advantages and disadvantages. They can provide critical start-up credit, but in order to obtain one, your personal credit will need to be good, and you will, of course, have to pay them off with interest. In general, the more you and your partners put into the business yourselves, the more credit lenders will be willing to extend to you.

Equity can come from your own personal investment, either in cash or an equity loan on your home. You may also want to consider bringing on partners—at least limited financial partners—as a way to cover start-up costs.

It is also worth considering obtaining a line of credit instead of a loan. A loan is taken out all at once, but with a line of credit, you draw on the money as you need it. This both saves you interest payments and means that you have the money you need when you need it. Taking out too large of a loan can be worse than having no money at all! It just sits there collecting interest—or, worse, is spent on something utterly un-necessary—and then is not around when you need it most.

The first five years are the hardest for any business venture; your venture has about double the usual chance of closing in this time (1 out of 6, rather than 1 out of 12). You will probably have to tighten your belt at home, as well as work long hours and keep careful track of your business expenses. Be careful with your money. Do not take unnecessary risks, play it conservatively, and always keep some capital in reserve for emergencies. The hardest part of a new business, of course, is the learning curve of figuring out what, exactly, you need to do to make a profit, and so the best advice is to have plenty of savings—or a job to provide income—while you learn the ropes.

One thing you should not do is count on venture capitalists or "angel investors," that is, businesspeople who make a living investing on other businesses in the hopes that their equity in the company will increase in value. Venture capitalists have gotten something of a reputation as indiscriminate spendthrifts due to some poor choices made during the dot-com boom of the late 1990s, but the fact is that most do not take risks on unproven products. Rather, they are attracted to young companies that have the potential to become regional or national powerhouses and give better-than-average returns. Nor are venture capitalists endless sources of money; rather, they are savvy businesspeople who are usually attracted to companies that have already experienced a measure of success. Therefore, it is better to rely on your own resources until you have proven your business will work.

Bookkeeping 101

The principles of double-entry bookkeeping have not changed much since its invention in the fifteenth century: one column records debits, and one records credits. The trick is *doing* it. As a small business owner, you need to be disciplined and meticulous at recording your finances. Thankfully, today there is software available that can do everything from tracking payables and receivables to running checks and generating reports.

Honestly ask yourself if you are the sort of person who does a good job keeping track of finances. If you are not, outsource to a bookkeeping company or hire someone to come in once or twice a week to enter invoices and generate checks for you. Also remember that if you have employees or even freelancers, you will have to file tax forms for them at the end of the year.

Another good idea is to have an accountant for your business to handle advice and taxes (federal, state, local, sales tax, etc.). In fact, consulting with a certified public accountant is a good idea in general, since they are usually aware of laws and rules that you have never even heard of.

Finally, keep your personal and business accounting separate. If your business ever gets audited, the first thing the IRS looks for is personal expenses disguised as business expenses. A good accountant can help you to know what are legitimate business expenses. Everything you take from the business account, such as payroll and reimbursement, must be recorded and classified.

Being an Employer

Know your situation regarding employees. To begin with, if you have any employees, you will need an Employer Identification Number (EIN), also sometimes called a Federal Tax Identification Number. Getting an EIN is simple: You can fill out IRS form SS-4, or complete the process online at http://www.irs.gov.

Having employees carries other responsibilities and legalities with it. To begin with, you will need to pay payroll taxes (otherwise known as "withholding") to cover income tax, unemployment insurance, Social Security, and Medicare, as well as file W-2 and W-4 forms with the government. You will also be required to pay worker's compensation insurance, and will probably also want to find medical insurance. You are also required to abide by your state's nondiscrimination laws. Most states require you to post nondiscrimination and compensation notices in a public area.

Many employers are tempted to unofficially hire workers "off the books." This can have advantages, but can also mean entering a legal gray area. (Note, however, this is different from hiring freelancers, a temp employed by another company, or having a self-employed professional such as an accountant or bookkeeper come in occasionally to provide a service.) It is one thing to hire the neighbor's teenage son on a one-time basis to help you move some boxes, but quite another to have full-time workers working on a cash-and-carry basis. Regular wages must be noted in the accounts, and gaps may be questioned in the event of an audit. If the workers are injured on the job, you are not covered by worker's comp, and are thus vulnerable to lawsuits. If the workers you hired are not legal residents, you can also be liable for civil and criminal penalties. In general, it is best to keep your employees as above-board as possible.

Building a Business

Good business practices are essential to success. First off, do not overextend yourself. Be honest about what you can do and in what time frame. Secondly, be a responsible business owner. In general, if there is a problem, it is best to explain matters honestly to your clients than to leave them without word and wondering. In the former case, there is at least the possibility of salvaging your reputation and credibility.

Most business is still built by personal contacts and word of mouth. It is for this reason that maintaining your list of contacts is an essential practice. Even if a particular contact may not be useful at a particular moment, a future opportunity may present itself—or you may be able to send someone else to them. Networking, in other words, is as important when you are the boss as when you are looking for a job yourself. As the owner of a company, having a network means getting services on better terms, knowing where to go if you need help with a particular problem, or simply being in the right place at the right time to exploit an opportunity. Join professional organizations, the local Chamber of Commerce, clubs and community organizations, and learn to play golf. And remember—never burn a bridge.

Advertising is another way to build a business. Planning an ad campaign is not as difficult as you might think: You probably already know your media market and business community. The trick is applying it. Again, go with your instincts. If you never look twice at your local weekly, other people probably do not, either. If you are in a high-tourist area, though, local tourist maps might be a good way to leverage your marketing dollar. Ask other people in your area or market who have businesses similar to your own. Depending on your focus, you might want to consider everything from AM radio or local TV networks, to national trade publications, to hiring a PR firm for an all-out blitz. By thinking about these questions, you can spend your advertising dollars most effectively.

Nor should you underestimate the power of using the Internet to build your business. It is a very powerful tool for small businesses, potentially reaching vast numbers of people for relatively little outlay of money. Launching a Web site has become the modern equivalent of hanging out your shingle. Even if you are primarily a brick-and-mortar business, a Web presence can still be an invaluable tool—your store or offices will show up on Google searches, plus customers can find directions to visit you in person. Furthermore, the Internet offers the small-business owner many useful tools. Print and design services, order fulfillment, credit card processing, and networking—both personal and in terms of linking to other sites—are all available online. Web advertising can be useful, too, either by advertising on specialty sites that appeal to your audience, or by using services such as Google AdWords.

Amateurish print ads, TV commercials, and Web sites do not speak well of your business. Good media should be well-designed, well-edited, and well-put together. It need not, however, be expensive. Shop around and, again, use your network.

Flexibility is also important. "In general, a business must adapt to changing conditions, find new customers and find new products or services that customers need when the demand for their older products or services diminishes," says James Peck, a Long Island, New York, entrepreneur. In other words, if your original plan is not working out, or if demand falls, see if you can parlay your experience, skills, and physical plant into meeting other needs. People are not the only ones who can change their path in life; organizations can, too.

A Final Word

In business, as in other areas of life, the advice of more experienced people is essential. "I think it really takes three businesses until you know what you're doing," Drew Curtis confides. "I sure didn't know what I was doing the first time." Listen to what others have to say, no matter whether it is about your Web site or your business plan. One possible solution is seeking out a mentor, someone who has previously launched a successful venture in this field. In any case, before taking any step, ask as many people as many questions as you can. Good advice is invaluable.

Further Resources

American Independent Business Alliance
http://www.amiba.net

American Small Business League
http://www.asbl.com

IRS Small Business and Self-Employed One-Stop Resource
http://www.irs.gov/businesses/small/index.html

The Riley Guide: Steps in Starting Your Own Business
http://www.rileyguide.com/steps.html

Small Business Administration
http://www.sba.gov

Appendix B

Outfitting Yourself for Career Success

As you contemplate a career shift, the first component is to assess your interests. You need to figure out what makes you tick, since there is a far greater chance that you will enjoy and succeed in a career that taps into your passions, inclinations, natural abilities, and training. If you have a general idea of what your interests are, you at least know in which direction you want to travel. You may know you want to simply switch from one sort of nursing to another, or change your life entirely and pursue a dream you have always held. In this case, you can use a specific volume of The Field Guides to Finding a New Career to discover which position to target. If you are unsure of the direction you want to take, well, then the entire scope of the series is open to you! Browse through to see what appeals to you, and see if it matches with your experience and abilities.

The next step you should take is to make a list—do it once in writing—of the skills you have used in a position of responsibility that transfer to the field you are entering. People in charge of interviewing and hiring may well understand that the skills they are looking for in a new hire are used in other fields, but you must spell it out. Most job descriptions are partly a list of skills. Map your experience into that, and very early in your contacts with a prospective employer explicitly address how you acquired your relevant skills. Pick a relatively unimportant aspect of the job to be your ready answer for where you would look forward to learning within the organization, if this seems essentially correct. When you transfer into a field, softly acknowledge a weakness while relating your readiness to learn, but never lose sight of the value you offer both in your abilities and in the freshness of your perspective.

Energy and Experience

The second component in career-switching success is energy. When Jim Fulmer was 61, he found himself forced to close his piano-repair business. However, he was able to parlay his knowledge of music, pianos, and the musical instruments industry into another job as a sales representative for a large piano manufacturer, and quickly built up a clientele of musical-instrument retailers throughout the East Coast. Fulmer's experience highlights another essential lesson for career-changers: There are plenty of opportunities out there, but jobs will not come to you—especially the career-oriented, well-paying ones. You have to seek them out.

Jim Fulmer's case also illustrates another important point: Former training and experience can be a key to success. "Anyone who has to make a career change in any stage of life has to look at what skills they have acquired but may not be aware of," he says. After all, people can more easily change into careers similar to the ones they are leaving. Training and experience also let you enter with a greater level of seniority, provided you have the other necessary qualifications. For instance, a nurse who is already experienced with administering drugs and their benefits and drawbacks, and who is also graced with the personality and charisma to work with the public, can become a pharmaceutical company sales representative.

Unlock Your Network

The next step toward unlocking the perfect job is networking. The term may be overused, but the idea is as old as civilization. More than other animals, humans need one another. With the Internet and telephone, never in history has it been easier to form (or revive) these essential links. One does not have to gird oneself and attend reunion-type events (though for many this is a fine tactic)—but keep open to opportunities to meet people who may be friendly to you in your field. Ben Franklin understood the principle well—*Poor Richard's Almanac* is something of a treatise on the importance of cultivating what Franklin called "friendships" with benefactors. So follow in the steps of the founding fathers and make friends to get ahead. Remember: helping others feels good; it's often the receiving that gets a little tricky. If you know someone particularly well-connected in your field, consider tapping one or two less important connections first so that you make the most of the important one. As you proceed, keep your strengths foremost in your mind because the glue of commerce is mutual interest.

Eighty percent of job openings are *never advertised*, and, according to the U.S. Bureau of Labor statistics, more than half of all employees landed their jobs through networking. Using your personal contacts is far more efficient and effective than trusting your résumé to the Web. On the Web, an employer needs to sort through tens of thousands—or millions—of résumés. When you direct your application to one potential employer, you are directing your inquiry to one person who already knows you. The personal touch is everything: Human beings are social animals, programmed to "read" body language; we are naturally inclined to trust those we meet in person, or who our friends and coworkers have recommended. While Web sites can be useful (for looking through help-wanted ads, for instance), expecting employers to pick you out of the slush pile is as effective as throwing your résumé into a black hole.

Do not send your résumé out just to make yourself feel like you're doing something. The proper way to go about things is to employ discipline and order, and then to apply your charm. Begin your networking efforts by making a list of people you can talk to: colleagues, coworkers, and supervisors, people you have had working relationship with, people from church, athletic teams, political organizations, or other community groups, friends, and relatives. You can expand your networking opportunities by following the suggestions in each chapter of the volumes. Your goal here is not so much to land a job as to expand your possibilities and knowledge: Though the people on your list may not be in the position to help you themselves, they might know someone who is. Meeting with them might also help you understand traits that matter and skills that are valued in the field in which you are interested. Even if the person is a potential employer, it is best to phrase your request as if you were seeking information: "You might not be able to help me, but do you know someone I could talk to who could tell me more about what it is like to work in this field?" Being hungry gives one impression, being desperate quite another.

Keep in mind that networking is a two-way street. If you meet someone who has an opening that is not right for you, but you could recommend someone else, you have just added to your list two people who will be favorably disposed toward you in the future. Also, bear in mind that *you* can help people in *your* old field, thus adding to your own contacts list.

Networking is especially important to the self-employed or those who start their own businesses. Many people in this situation begin because they either recognize a potential market in a field that they are familiar with, or because full-time employment in this industry is no longer a possibility. Already being well-established in a field can help, but so can asking connections for potential work and generally making it known that you are ready, willing, and able to work. Working your professional connections, in many cases, is the *only* way to establish yourself. A freelancer's network, in many cases, is like a spider's web. The spider casts out many strands, since he or she never knows which one might land the next meal.

Dial-Up Help

In general, it is better to call contacts directly than to e-mail them. E-mails are easy for busy people to ignore or overlook, even if they do not mean to. Explain your situation as briefly as possible (see the discussion of the "elevator speech"), and ask if you could meet briefly, either at their office or at a neutral place such as a café. (Be sure that you pay the bill in such a situation—it is a way of showing you appreciate their time and effort.) If you get someone's voicemail, give your "elevator speech" and then say you will call back in a few days to follow up—and then do so. If you reach your contact directly and they are too busy to speak or meet with you, make a definite appointment to call back at a later date. Be persistent, but not annoying.

Once you have arranged a meeting, prep yourself. Look at industry publications both in print and online, as well as news reports (here, GoogleNews, which lets you search through online news reports, can be very handy). Having up-to-date information on industry trends shows that you are dedicated, knowledgeable, and focused. Having specific questions on employers and requests for suggestions will set you apart from the rest of the job-hunting pack. Knowing the score—for instance, asking about the value of one sort of certification instead of another— pegs you as an "insider," rather than a dilettante, someone whose name is worth remembering and passing along to a potential employer.

Finally, set the right mood. Here, a little self-hypnosis goes a long way: Look at yourself in the mirror, and tell yourself that you are an enthusiastic, committed professional. Mood affects confidence and performance. Discipline your mind so you keep your perspective and self-respect. Nobody wants to hire someone who comes across as insincere, tells a sob story, or is still in the doldrums of having lost their previous job. At the end of any networking meeting, ask for someone else who might be able to help you in your journey to finding a position in this field, either with information or a potential job opening.

Get a Lift

When you meet with a contact in person (as well as when you run into anyone by chance who may be able to help you), you need an "elevator speech" (so-named because it should be short enough to be delivered during an elevator ride from a ground level to a high floor). This is a summary in which, in less than two minutes, you give them a clear impression of who you are, where you come from, your experience and goals, and why you are on the path you are on. The motto above Plato's Academy holds true: Know Thyself (this is where our Career Compasses and guides will help you). A long and rambling "elevator story" will get you nowhere. Furthermore, be positive: Neither a sad-sack story nor a tirade explaining how everything that went wrong in your old job is someone else's fault will get you anywhere. However, an honest explanation of a less-than-fortunate circumstance, such as a decline in business forcing an office closure, needing to change residence to a place where you are not qualified to work in order to further your spouse's career, or needing to work fewer hours in order to care for an ailing family member, is only honest.

An elevator speech should show 1) you know the business involved; 2) you know the company; 3) you are qualified (here, try to relate your education and work experience to the new situation); and 4) you are goal-oriented, dependable, and hardworking. Striking a balance is important; you want to sound eager, but not overeager. You also want to show a steady work experience, but not that you have been so narrowly focused that you cannot adjust. Most important is emphasizing what you can do for the company. You will be surprised how much information you can include in two minutes. Practice this speech in front of a mirror until you have the key points down perfectly. It should sound natural, and you should come across as friendly, confident, and assertive. Finally, remember eye contact! Good eye contact needs to be part of your presentation, as well as your everyday approach when meeting potential employers and leads.

Get Your Résumé Ready

Everyone knows what a résumé is, but how many of us have really thought about how to put one together? Perhaps no single part of the job search is subject to more anxiety—or myths and misunderstandings—than this 8 ½-by-11-inch sheet of paper.

On the one hand, it is perfectly all right for someone—especially in certain careers, such as academia—to have a résumé that is more than one page. On the other hand, you do not need to tell a future employer *everything*. Trim things down to the most relevant; for a 40-year-old to mention an internship from two decades ago is superfluous. Likewise, do not include irrelevant jobs, lest you seem like a professional career-changer.

Tailor your descriptions of your former employment to the particular position you are seeking. This is not to say you should lie, but do make your experience more appealing. If the job you're looking for involves supervising other people, say if you have done this in the past; if it involves specific knowledge or capabilities, mention that you possess these qualities. In general, try to make your past experience seem similar to what you are seeking.

The standard advice is to put your Job Objective at the heading of the résumé. An alternative to this is a Professional Summary, which some recruiters and employers prefer. The difference is that a Job Objective mentions the position you are seeking, whereas a Professional Summary mentions your background (e.g. "Objective: To find a position as a sales representative in agribusiness machinery" versus "Experienced sales representative; strengths include background in agribusiness, as well as building team dynamics and market expansion"). Of course, it is easy to come up with two or three versions of the same document for different audiences.

The body of the résumé of an experienced worker varies a lot more than it does at the beginning of your career. You need not put your education or your job experience first; rather, your résumé should emphasize your strengths. If you have a master's degree in a related field, that might want to go before your unrelated job experience. Conversely, if too much education will harm you, you might want to bury that under the section on professional presentations you have given that show how good you are at communicating. If you are currently enrolled in a course or other professional development, be sure to note this (as well as your date of expected graduation). A résumé is a study of blurs, highlights, and jewels. You blur everything you must in order to fit the description of your experience to the job posting. You highlight what is relevant from each and any of your positions worth mentioning. The jewels are the little headers and such—craft them, since they are what is seen first.

You may also want to include professional organizations, work-related achievements, and special abilities, such as your fluency in a foreign language. Also mention your computer software qualifications and capabilities, especially if you are looking for work in a technological field or if you are an older job-seeker who might be perceived as behind the technology curve. Including your interests or family information might or might not be a good idea—no one really cares about your bridge club, and in fact they might worry that your marathon training might take away from your work commitments, but, on the other hand, mentioning your golf handicap or three children might be a good idea if your potential employer is an avid golfer or is a family woman herself.

You can either include your references or simply note, "References available upon request." However, be sure to ask your references' permission to use their names and alert them to the fact that they may be contacted before you include them on your résumé! Be sure to include name, organization, phone number, and e-mail address for each contact.

Today, word processors make it easy to format your résumé. However, beware of prepackaged résumé "wizards"—they do not make you stand out in the crowd. Feel free to strike out on your own, but remember the most important thing in formatting a résumé is consistency. Unless you have a background in typography, do not get too fancy. Finally, be sure to have someone (or several people!) read your résumé over for you.

For more information on résumé writing, check out Web sites such as http://www.résumé.monster.com.

Craft Your Cover Letter

It is appropriate to include a cover letter with your résumé. A cover letter lets you convey extra information about yourself that does not fit or is not always appropriate in your résumé, such as why you are no longer working in your original field of employment. You can and should also mention the name of anyone who referred you to the job. You can go into some detail about the reason you are a great match, given the job description. Also address any questions that might be raised in the potential employer's mind (for instance, a gap in employment). Do not, however, ramble on. Your cover letter should stay focused on your goal: To offer a strong, positive impression of yourself and persuade the hiring manager that you are worth an interview. Your cover letter gives you a chance to stand out from the other applicants and sell yourself. In fact, according to a CareerBuilder.com survey, 23 percent of hiring managers say a candidate's ability to relate his or her experience to the job at hand is a top hiring consideration.

Even if you are not a great writer, you can still craft a positive yet concise cover letter in three paragraphs: An introduction containing the specifics of the job you are applying for; a summary of why you are a good fit for the position and what you can do for the company; and a closing with a request for an interview, contact information, and thanks. Remember to vary the structure and tone of your cover letter—do not begin every sentence with "I."

Ace Your Interview

In truth, your interview begins well before you arrive. Be sure to have read up well on the company and its industry. Use Web sites and magazines—http://www.hoovers.com offers free basic business information, and trade magazines deliver both information and a feel for the industries they cover. Also, do not neglect talking to people in your circle who might know about trends in the field. Leave enough time to digest the information so that you can give some independent thought to the company's history and prospects. You don't need to be an expert when you arrive to be interviewed; but you should be comfortable. The most important element of all is to be poised and relaxed during the interview itself. Preparation and practice can help a lot.

Be sure to develop well-thought-through answers to the following, typical interview openers and standard questions.

☞ Tell me about yourself. (Do not complain about how unsatisfied you were in your former career, but give a brief summary

of your applicable background and interest in the particular job area.) If there is a basis to it, emphasize how much
you love to work and how you are a team player.

☞ Why do you want this job? (Speak from the brain, and the heart—of
course you want the money, but say a little here about what you
find interesting about the field and the company's role in it.)

☞ What makes you a good hire? (Remember here to connect the
company's needs and your skill set. Ultimately, your selling
points probably come down to one thing: you will make your employer money. You want the prospective hirer to see that your
skills are valuable not to the world in general but to this specific company's bottom line. What can you do for them?)

☞ What led you to leave your last job? (If you were fired, still try to say
something positive, such as, "The business went through a challenging time, and some of the junior marketing people were let go.")

Practice answering these and other questions, and try to be genuinely positive about yourself, and patient with the process. Be secure but
not cocky; don't be shy about forcing the focus now and then on positive
contributions you have made in your working life—just be specific. As
with the elevator speech, practice in front of the mirror.

A couple pleasantries are as natural a way as any to start the actual
interview, but observe the interviewer closely for any cues to fall silent
and formally begin. Answer directly; when in doubt, finish your phrase
and look to the interviewer. Without taking command, you can always
ask, "Is there more you would like to know?" Your attentiveness will convey respect. Let your personality show too—a positive attitude and a
grounded sense of your abilities will go a long way to getting you considered. During the interview, keep your cell phone off and do not look at
your watch. Toward the end of your meeting, you may be asked whether
you have any questions. It is a good idea to have one or two in mind. A
few examples follow:

☞ "What makes your company special in the field?"

☞ "What do you consider the hardest part of this position?"

☞ "Where are your greatest opportunities for growth?"

☞ "Do you know when you might need anything further from me?"

Leave discussion of terms for future conversations. Make a cordial, smooth exit.

Remember to Follow Up

Send a thank-you note. Employers surveyed by CareerBuilder.com in 2005 said it matters. About 15 percent said they would not hire someone who did not follow up with a thanks. And almost 33 percent would think less of a candidate. The form of the note does not much matter—if you know a manager's preference, use it. Otherwise, just be sure to follow up.

Winning an Offer

A job offer can feel like the culmination of a long and difficult struggle. So naturally, when you hear them, you may be tempted to jump at the offer. Don't. Once an employer wants you, he or she will usually give you a chance to consider the offer. This is the time to discuss terms of employment, such as vacation, overtime, and benefits. A little effort now can be well worth it in the future. Be sure to do a check of prevailing salaries for your field and area before signing on. Web sites for this include Payscale.com, Salary.com, and Salaryexpert.com. If you are thinking about asking for better or different terms from what the prospective employer offered, rest assured—that's how business gets done; and it may just burnish the positive impression you have already made.